The Trauma of Transparency

A Biblical Approach to Inter-Personal Communication

by

J. Grant Howard

MULTNOMAH PRESS
PORTLAND, OREGON 97266

Cover design and illustration: Britt Taylor Collins
Illustrations: Ruth Korch

THE TRAUMA OF TRANSPARENCY
© 1979 by Multnomah Press
Portland, Oregon 97266

Printed in the United States of America

Third Printing 1982

Library of Congress Cataloging in Publication Data

Howard, J Grant
    The trauma of transparency: a biblical approach to interpersonal communication / by J. Grant Howard; [ill., Ruth Korch].—Portland, Or.: Multnomah Press, © 1979.

    235 p.: ill.; 23cm.

    Includes bibliographies and indexes.
    1. Communication (Theology)   2. Interpersonal relations.
    I. Title.
BV4319.H63   248.4   79-125709
ISBN 0-930014-28-6 (hdbk.)
ISBN 0-930014-73-1 (pbk.)

To Audrey
Jim
Beth
Jeanne
and
Juli

Preface

*E*vangelicals need to develop a biblical theology of inter-personal communication. This book is written to contribute to that goal. It is a biblically-centered, life-related approach to the subject. Those who are interested in further study and communication of these concepts will want to consult the material at the end of each chapter.

My thanks to Donna Randall and Lynn Strutton for their precision typing. To Mike Winter, Kem Oberholtzer, Patti Heuton and Debby Anderson for their help with the graphics. A special word of appreciation to Ruth Korch who drew the illustrations. She has an uncanny ability to visualize verbal concepts. The scenes in chapter four are prime examples of her skill. I am grateful to Western Conservative Baptist Seminary for providing the resources, the time and the encouragement to engage in this research and writing.

—J. Grant Howard
Portland, Oregon

Table of Contents

Prologue

*M*eet Chuck and Patty. They're getting along well. You can tell by observing them.

They're looking at each other.
They're touching.
They're smiling.
They're talking.
And you know
how they feel.
They feel good.
About
themselves.
About each other.
About their
relationship.

They are happy.

How long will it last?

It will last until...

...they get upset with each other and start saying things like—

"You didn't even offer to help me in the kitchen Thursday night. You never do."

"You were way too easy on Chuckie this morning when he disobeyed you. You always are."

And as a result of these words, you know how they feel. Bad. About themselves. About each other. About their relationship. They aren't happy.

So they turn away from each other. Retreating into a moody, sulky silence.

Each waiting for the other to say "I'm sorry." In the meantime, you know how they feel. Not good. They aren't happy.

THE QUESTION IS........

WHY?   Why can't Chuck and Patty and all the rest of us always say the right words in the right way at the right time...so we'll always feel good about ourselves and each other and our relationships... so we'll always be happy?
What's wrong with us?
What's our problem?

HOW?   How can Chuck and Patty and all the rest of us do a better job of communicating with each other...so we can feel good...so we can be happy?
What's the answer?
What's the solution?

The rest of this book is designed to probe for the answers to these questions.

Come on...let's communicate!

Part 1
Examining the Problem

Chapter 1

The Transparent Couple

I can relate in a fairly meaningful way to a beautiful sunset, a medium-rare steak, a salary check and a radial arm saw. But I can communicate in a much more meaningful way with my wife, my four children, my parents, my colleagues at work, and my students in class. Why? I am a person. Sunsets, steaks, salaries and saws are not persons. Wives, children, parents and friends are. Persons *relate* to things. Persons *communicate* with persons.

Communication between God and Man

God is a person. He relates to His world of nature in a meaningful way, but He communicates to the people in that world in a vastly different and much more profound way—because we are persons. We are going to examine Genesis 1 and 2. In this portion of Scripture, note that God talks *about* His world of nature, but He goes a step further and talks *with* the people in that world.

God is a personal being with the capacity to communicate. He created man in His image. Man, therefore, is a personal being with the same capacity to communicate. Like his Creator he can think, feel and decide. These elements of personality are what Dwight Small calls "relational bridges" through which an intimate union with God is possible.[1] Nothing else in God's creation, even though it be alive, has this kind of personhood. Only man is a person and can engage in the communication process with his Creator.

That man was created to have this personal, intimate relationship with God is never really explicitly stated in Genesis 1 and 2. It is assumed. But what is assumed in the creation account is explicitly revealed elsewhere. Man's problem is sin and sin *alienates* him from God. Alienation presupposes a prior relationship. The solution is *reconciliation*. Reconciliation allows for the original relationship to be restored. In Christ, man once again enters into a peaceful friendship with God.[2]

In Genesis 1 and 2 that peaceful friendship existed and thus God and man could and did have open, honest and appropriate communication with each other. Here we see the Father and His son before the son becomes a prodigal. We don't have the full transcript of what they said. There are a lot of divinely ordained "gaps" in the Eden tapes! But let us briefly analyze what *is* recorded.

After forming Adam, God took him on a guided tour of his new abode—the garden in Eden (Genesis 2:7-17). He told Adam that it was his responsibility to cultivate it and care for it. He also made it patently clear what the restrictions were. "See that tree over there? That is the tree of the knowledge of good and evil. Don't ever eat any fruit from that tree. It is off-limits. Forbidden!"

He then followed up with a concise statement of the consequences of disobedience. "If you eat fruit from that tree, you will most certainly die."

Adam was seeing and hearing all of this for the first time. I would imagine that he asked God to explain and amplify a number of things.

"Tell me more about that tree's 'No Trespassing' sign."
"What is the difference between good and evil?"
"What does it mean to 'die'?"

And I can't imagine God doing anything but graciously answering this inquisitive individual. Not that God would tell him everything, but how gladly He would talk with him.

It is obvious that God is a very precise, articulate communicator. Even in the garden He doesn't beat around the bush! "Don't ever eat any fruit from that tree." What is wrong is wrong. When involved in a conversation with God there are always some non-negotiable items. Some directive statements. Obedience is one of them.

In Genesis 2:18 God evaluates Adam's aloneness as "not good" and declares His intention to make a companion for him—one who would suitably fill his solitude. Note that God doesn't ask Adam's advice as to how to best meet this need. A sovereign, all-wise Creator already knows what is best for His creature. Sometimes the best way for needy people to dialogue with God is to listen.

At this point (Genesis 2:19-20), God involves Adam in a do-it-yourself project. Adam names all of the animals. In the process he discovers that none of them would be a suitable partner for him. Never tell a student that which he can learn for himself. That is a basic law in the teaching-learning process. It is not, however, inviolable. There are times when we do tell a student (especially a young child) something that he could learn on his own. But here God does employ that principle and allows Adam to draw an internalized conclusion that nothing in the animal kingdom could fully meet his need for companionship. It was a see-for-yourself project.

In Genesis 1:28-30 we are privileged to eavesdrop on what may have been the first words God shared with Adam and Eve. God "blessed" them. To "bless" is to bestow not only a gift, but a function.[3] When God blessed the man and the woman He did it by first telling them what their function would be—to fill the earth, subdue it and rule over it. Then he showed them that He had provided the gift of food for their health and growth so they could discharge these functions. The communication of vital information is one of the ways that God blesses. He did it with Adam and Eve. He does it with us today. His words to the first couple contained a concise statement of their responsibilities and their resources.

Is this all God said? Did He explain "fill," "subdue," and "rule"? Did He go over their food supply and give them insight on nutrition, diet, cooking and serving? Were Adam and Eve passive listeners who took it all in and then set out to function without any further interaction with and insight from their Creator?

Scripture is silent on these questions. We simply do not know how much communication took place between God and man before the fall. We don't know even how much time elapsed between the creation and the fall.

Let me suggest a point that may shed some light on the above questions. Throughout Scripture God is seen functioning as a Father who is deeply concerned about the security and growth of His children. He does this by telling us everything we *need* to know (cf. 2 Timothy 3:16-17). He does not tell us everything we *want* to know (cf. Deuteronomy 29:29). Adam and Eve undoubtedly needed to know many other things that are not recorded in Genesis 1 and 2, and I'm certain that God shared these things with them. But He didn't tell them everything—everything they could know or everything they wanted to know.

Children grow not only by *listening* and learning but also by *living* and learning. God undoubtedly allowed the first couple the privilege of discovering and developing their powers of discernment and decision. All their discernment and decisions would ultimately have had to be related to the truth that resides in the Father, but their relationship to the Father's truth could be explored and understood in the context of their experience as well as in personal dialogue with the Father prior to and after the experience. Adam and Eve learned many things by listening to God. They learned many other things by exploring and experimenting. The garden in Eden was not just a classroom; it was also a laboratory. God communicated many things to Adam and Eve before the fall, but not everything. God communicated many times to Adam

Unlimited Access to God

and Eve before the fall, but not all the time. He provided a context where they would feel secure and could grow—sheltered but not smothered.

As far as access to God is concerned, His eyes and ears are always open to His children (Psalm 34:15). We can assume that Adam and Eve had unlimited access to God. They could communicate with Him whenever they so desired.

Just as John 20:30 reveals that Jesus performed many other miracles than those which are recorded in John, so the author of Genesis could have said: "Many other conversations Adam and Eve had with their Lord, but these few are recorded so that you can catch a glimpse of the intimate fellowship that existed between them." The sound of the Lord God walking in the garden (Genesis 3:8) was one with which they were apparently quite familiar.

Communication between Adam and Eve

Without woman, man is classified as being "alone," a condition that God said was "not good" (Genesis 2:18). Man was made with both the capacity and the need to relate. Even though he had fellowship with his Creator, he still needed the companionship of another creature. Such a companion would be a "helper." The term refers to a beneficial relationship where one person aids or supports another person as a friend and ally. It does not signify a subordinate relationship. It is not saying that God will make a servant for Adam. This same Hebrew word is used when God Himself is referred to as *"a very present help in trouble"* (Psalm 46:1). Certainly He is not to be regarded as a subordinate to man!

"Suitable for him" highlights the fact that the forthcoming partner will correspond to as well as complement the man. None of the animals could do this. Only another one, like, yet opposite to him.

The woman, first and foremost, is to help the man's aloneness. She is to release him from his human solitary confinement and relate to him as a partner and companion—his divinely fashioned counterpart. When the newly-created woman is brought to the man, he responds to her with words that express a sense of deep, personal kinship. *"This is now bone of my bones, and flesh of my flesh"* (Genesis 2:23). This expression is frequently used in the Old Testament to designate intimate, personal relationship between individuals.[4] Adam, however, could employ these words in their full, literal connotation—the woman was actually bone of his bones and flesh of his flesh!

Along with a recognition of intimate kinship, there is an expression of excitement in Adam's words. The sense is: "This creature, this time (that is, at last), is in truth a helper corresponding to me!"[5] He looked upon her as a person, not a thing. He saw her in terms of unity, not utility. At last, someone to talk with, to listen to.

In Genesis 2:24 the marriage relationship is characterized as a joining of two so they become one. One essential ingredient involved in establishing, maintaining and developing that kind of unity is communication.

In Genesis 2:25 both partners are described as naked, yet without any sense of shame. This does not mean that they had no sexual desires. It simply means that they had not learned that sexual desire could be directed toward evil ends. They looked upon the sexual organs in the same way we regard the hands or the face. They were comfortable with each other. There were no barriers between them. They were ready, willing, able and needing to communicate with each other.

The fact that there were no barriers does not mean that they experienced some kind of instant intimacy with each other. Even though they weren't sinful, they still had to go through the process of getting to know one another; of adjusting to one another; of learning to live with one another. For us, in our sinfulness, that process is even more difficult and demanding. But Adam and Eve, even in their period of probationary perfection, were not exempt from the responsibility and challenge of developing their unity and harmony. Perfect people don't have instant, automatic relationships. They simply have the capacity to develop perfect relationships. Christ was a perfect person, yet He still went through the process of increasing in wisdom and stature and in favor with God and man (Luke 2:52). Adam and Eve had to do the same. As humans they had to grow up. As humans they had to grow together.

Take, for example, their first walk through the garden.

A: *"Just look at this garden. Isn't it beautiful?"*

E: *"Yes. The colors are luscious and the water is so cool and refreshing."*

A: *"This is our home. It is where we are going to live and work and eat and sleep."*

E: *"Speaking of eating, I'm hungry. Let's have lunch."*

A: *"I'm going to have some of these berries. Say, they are really good. Here, try some."*

E: *"Okay—Hey, they're a bit tart for me. I'm not sure I like them."*

All of a sudden, we have a difference of opinion. Not that one is right and the other is wrong. They are just different. Sinless people (and even sanctified saints) can and will have legitimate differences of opinion. You discover these differences and learn to live with them through the medium of good communication.

A: *"What shall we do today?"*

E: *"I don't care. Anything you want to do is fine with me."*

A: *"How about picking some fruit?"*

E: *"Well, I guess we could, but we also need to dig around the lettuce and prune the cherry trees."*

Decisions. Decisions. Even Adam and Eve had to make them. Decisions are made in the context of communication. It is very easy to come up with the idea that perfect people will have an automatic, decision-free life. Not so. Christ lived a perfect life, but one can't read the gospels and conclude that His was a sterile, robot-like lifestyle. He discussed things; He had differences of opinion (even with his mother, Luke 2:48-49); He made decisions (Mark 1:38).

They were made to relate to each other and they enjoyed the luxury of open, honest, appropriate communication with each other. They did this as whole persons—mentally, emotionally, volitionally, socially, and sexually. It was the communication process that facilitated the unity they were

Open Communication with Each Other

developing. Beautifully, though undoubtedly briefly, Adam and Eve modeled their Creator, for just as God is a tri-unity of divine persons in relation, so man and woman were a bi-unity of human persons in relation.[6]

The garden scene was unique in the annals of human history. God and man involved in totally open and honest communication with one another. Man and woman doing the same on the horizontal level. Each saying what needed to be said—in the right way, at the right time, and for the right purpose. Here, for the moment, was that delicately balanced combination of truth and transparency that the world now struggles to understand and achieve. Each shared appropriate truth with the other. Each maintained the appropriate transparency with the other. The rest of this book develops how this communication pattern was lost and how in Christ it can be regained.

Interaction

1. Using the two diagrams in this chapter, can you briefly and concisely summarize the contents of the chapter?

2. Before the fall, Adam and Eve did not argue. Do you agree?

3. You may want to use your imagination and develop some more God-man or man-woman communication scenes in the garden. They could be role-played in a teaching situation.

4. Can Christians today have the same kind of communication relationship with God and each other that Adam and Eve had in the garden?

Footnotes

[1]Dwight Hervey Small, *Christian: Celebrate Your Sexuality* (Old Tappan, NJ: Fleming H. Revell Company, 1974), pp. 115-125. Small discusses six of these relational bridges (intelligence, emotionality, choice, values, self-consciousness, immortal spirit), showing how each is pertinent to both the God-man and man-woman relationship.

[2]For alienation see Ephesians 4:18 and Colossians 1:21. For reconciliation, see Romans 5:10; 2 Corinthians 5:18-21 and Colossians 1:20. Reconciliation is a doctrine that highlights the relational aspects of man's sin and God's salvation. One of the best studies on this subject is by Leon Morris, *The Apostolic Preaching of the Cross* (Grand Rapids: Wm. B. Eerdmans Publishing Co., 1955), pp. 186-223.

[3]In Genesis 1:22 God outlines the multiplying function of the fish and birds in His blessing. In 2:3 He sets aside the seventh day with His blessing—to function as a day of rest. In Numbers 6:24-26 God's blessing emphasizes the gift of His personal presence with Israel: "The Lord bless you, and...make His face shine on you."

[4]Genesis 29:14; Judges 9:2; 2 Samuel 5:1.

[5]This is the translation given by U. Cassuto (I, 135). Cassuto was a conservative Jewish scholar and any student familiar with the Hebrew language will do well to consult his two volumes on Genesis. *A Commentary on the Book of Genesis,* trans. Israel Abrahams (2 vols.; Jerusalem: The Magnes Press, The Hebrew University, 1944).

[6]Small, p. 130. The author briefly but cogently shows how the Trinity (three beings-in-relation) is the original model for the man-woman relationship.

Resources

Along with the works referred to in the footnotes, the following are suggested for additional insight on Genesis 1 and 2:

Jewett, Paul K. *Man as Male and Female.* Grand Rapids: Wm. B. Eerdmans Publishing Company, 1975.

Kidner, Derek. *Genesis.* London: The Tyndale Press, 1967.

Leupold, H.C. *Exposition of Genesis.* 2 vols. Grand Rapids: Baker Book House, 1960.

Stigers, Harold G. *A Commentary on Genesis.* Grand Rapids: Zondervan Publishing House, 1976.

Young, E.J. *In the Beginning.* Edinburgh, Scotland: The Banner of Truth Trust, 1976.

Chapter 2

The Traumatic Breakdown

*A*lice said, "My approach is to put up with it as long as I can, then when I can't take it any longer, I explode."

"And I usually get hit when she explodes," commented her husband, Tony. "I don't function that way. I say exactly what I think. And I get it off my chest as quickly as I can."

Why do Tony and Alice communicate like they do? Which one is right? The answers to these questions are found in Genesis 3. We are going to examine parts of this pivotal chapter to see what it has to say about communication.

Genesis 3:1-6—The Temptation and Fall

Satan, the crafty con-artist of the cosmos, goes to work on the innocent couple. He seeks to lead them to the point where they will willfully disobey their Creator. Speaking through one of the animals, a serpent, he appeals to their human capacity to think, feel and decide.

His communication has a built-in bias. He is anti-God and pro-self. Thus, the data he distributes is loaded with lies. He does not communicate to edify but to deceive. He does not seek to answer questions, but to raise them. He does not want to solve problems, but to create them. He casts doubt

on God's words: "Has God said...?" He issues an outright
denial of God's truth: "You surely shall not die." All of this
communication is designed to tempt the woman and man to
assert their wills against God.

And they did. They did what God told them not to do.
The results of their disobedience—*separation.* From
God. From each other. From their environment.

The Bible says you reap what you sow. In this situation
the crop came up immediately. Our transparent parents experienced a full-scale breakdown in their relationship with
God and each other. Let's analyze what happened.

Genesis 3:7-11—The Tendency to Hide

> 3:7 *"Then the eyes of both of them were opened,*
> *and they knew that they were naked; and they*
> *sewed fig leaves together and made themselves*
> *loin coverings."*

Their eyes were opened. Their perception of themselves
and of each other was changed. Before, they saw everything
as God saw it—good. Now they have an awareness that is
perverted and distorted. They are ill at ease with each other.
They are beginning to experience fallen human relationships.
They can no longer be open and honest with each other. Even
their sexuality is interpreted from a fallen human perspective.
They seek to cover themselves. They want to hide from each
other. The text refers to the creation of clothing to cover their
physical bodies, but we know that sin affected the total person. From that moment on, they tended to *hide* from one
another as persons. Man began to wear a mask. To fashion a
facade.

Many terms are used to depict this tendency we all have
to hide from one another. We cover up our needs. We bury
our thoughts. We repress our feelings. We mull things over
inwardly. We are quiet, reserved, or even withdrawn. We are
introverted. Sullen. Pouting. Shy. Bashful. We say, "I
couldn't care less," but we really do. We say, "Leave me

alone," because we don't want anyone to step inside and see what is really happening. We say, "I don't want to talk about it," even though we desperately need to. We say, "Nothing is bothering me," when in all honesty a problem is clawing our soul to shreds. We say, "I can work this out by myself," when in reality we can't; we need help.

We may pride ourselves on the ability to be open and honest in our relationships, and in certain situations and at certain times, we are. But basically we are sinners. Sinners tend to hide. Not simply because we are fearful, bashful, inarticulate and confused, but ultimately because we are sinners. Sin separates. Sin alienates. Sin causes people to hide from one another.

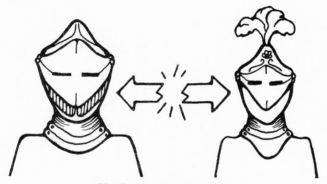

Sin Causes People to Hide

The man and the woman have put on their armor, depicting the propensity to hide and pretend. The real person, and all that is true of that person—both the good truth and the bad truth—tends to be hidden behind a superficial and, at times, even artificial disguise.

The disguise hides what really is inside. The real me. It also presents to others what I want to be, what I want others to see and hear and think about me. A decoy I use a lot is one of calmness and respectability. What's yours?

We are not saying that we hide everything; but that we *tend* to hide. Nor are we saying that we should be totally transparent and hide nothing. The solution to the problem of hiding is not telling everyone everything all of the time. We are going to work on the solution later. Right now we are focusing on the problem.

Adam and Eve sinned. An immediate, automatic reaction was to begin to withdraw from one another. Sin caused a breakdown in their communication with each other. Sinners tend to hide from each other.

> 3:8 *"And they heard the sound of the Lord God walking in the garden in the cool of the day, and the man and his wife hid themselves from the presence of the Lord God among the trees of the garden."*

It was time for His normal daily interaction with them. In the past they would have eagerly greeted Him. Now things were different. They react to Him just as they reacted to each other. They look for a hiding place. They no longer feel com-

Sin Severs the Relationship with God

fortable in open fellowship with Him. They don't want to communicate with Him. Guilty people never feel totally at ease with their accuser. The one who is unclean doesn't feel comfortable in the presence of Him who is spotless. When confrontation with your Creator (or any other significant person) appears to be forthcoming, the natural reaction of the sinner is to hide. Separation has occurred between God and man. The Creator and His creatures are no longer on speaking terms with each other. They are out of fellowship. Sinful man seeks to hide from a holy God.

The broken arrow in the diagram indicates a severed relationship. Man is now dead in trespasses and sins, alienated and hostile in his mind, and excluded from the life of God.[1]

The armor around man shows that he does not seek God, does not acknowledge God, does not honor God, worships and serves the creature (himself and others like him), rather than the Creator.[2] The breakdown in man's relationship with his Creator tends to bring about a corresponding build-up in man's relationship with himself. Separated man inevitably becomes self-centered man.[3] He avoids encounters with God. He keeps certain aspects of the truth at arms length, e.g. "What really is the world's problem?" "What really is my need?" "Honestly now, how good am I?" "Why am I here?" "Where am I going?"

The right answers to these questions call for some personal probing. Probing is both painful (when you don't like the answers) and humbling (when you don't know the answers and have to ask someone else). Man doesn't like to hurt or stoop. He thrives on pleasure and prestige.

Yet God relentlessly and lovingly seeks sinful man—as a shepherd seeks a lost sheep, as a woman seeks a lost coin, as a father seeks a lost son.[4] As God slips past man's outer defenses and begins to invade the real, inner person, man still desperately masks his basic problem and need. He hides behind his own background, his own works, or even his own (inexcusable) ignorance.[5]

Why does an intelligent person mislead himself—about himself and God? Simply this: nurtured by a satanically controlled world system, he is blind to the fact that he is deceiving himself and oblivious to the proposition that he is systematically involved in exchanging the truth of God for a lie.[6] He is so used to calling truth, error; and error, truth, that he has little awareness of the fact that he is engaged in a conspiracy to hide from God. Adam and Eve headed for the tall timber to hide from God. Modern man finds convenient cover or plants his own forests.

3:9 *"Then the Lord God called to the man, and said to him, 'Where are you?'"*

God takes the initiative to relate to man. He always does.[7] The question is not simply for information about man's location. God knew where he was. It was designed to confront him with his failure to appear and talk. "Where are you? What is the matter? Why aren't you meeting Me like usual?" Man doesn't want to talk with God. God is going to force him to, but He does it in a way that seeks to draw rather than drive him out of hiding.

3:10 *"And he said, 'I heard the sound of Thee in the garden, and I was afraid because I was naked; so I hid myself.'"*

Forced out of hiding, Adam stands shamefacedly before his Judge and mumbles his reply. These are the first recorded words of a sinner. Note how he communicates. He mixes truth—"I was afraid"—with half-truth—"because I was naked." The full truth was that he had disobeyed God and thus was aware of his nakedness. He did not level with God. He concealed his act of willfull disobedience instead of openly and honestly confessing it. Adam can no longer function as a completely authentic person. His capacity for credibility has plummeted downward. Sinners have trouble with truth. We can't tell it!

> 3:11 *"And He said, 'Who told you that you were
> naked? Have you eaten from the tree of which
> I commanded you not to eat?'"*

God presses him to be open and honest. He asks two
questions that probe the real Adam. God doesn't want to
play games. He wants to get at the truth. Adam has a chance
to offer a simple, direct confession. Now note how a sinner,
forced out of hiding and confronted with the truth,
communicates.

Genesis 3:12-13—The Tendency to Hurl

> 3:12 *"And the man said, 'The woman whom Thou
> gavest to be with me, she gave me from the
> tree, and I ate.'"*

Unable to hide any longer, Adam shifts the blame away
from himself to the woman and to God. "The *woman* whom
Thou gavest to be with me." He goes from hiding to *hurling*.
He hurls an accusation at his wife and then even seeks to im-
plicate his Creator.

Man Blames God and the Woman

In the span of a few brief moments sin has broken down the relationship between God and man; between man and his fellow man.

We hurl in a variety of ways. We act as judge and jury and condemn others. We project our problems on those who live with us. We ridicule. We dominate. We are dogmatic. We are sarcastic, obnoxious, overbearing. We pronounce the final word, when we have no reason nor right to. We cut a person down neatly with a word of criticism. To his face. Or behind his back. We nitpick at someone else's behavior patterns and often fail to acknowledge our own weaknesses. We say, "You never do anything right. You always forget." "Never" and "always" are super-sharp, expertly-barbed arrows from the hurler's communication quiver. We blame God. We blame others. We even blame ourselves.

Think, for example, of some of the ways we hurl at God. The sinner tells God what He is like and what He should be like. The sinner even tells God what he, the sinner, needs to do to have a personal relationship with God. The sinner periodically punctuates his conversation with God's name, using it in a variety of ways.

Sinners come in many forms. The *pantheist* has managed to integrate his god into nature so well that he does not have to worry about him. He can just enjoy him, worship him, cultivate him, and prune him—if he gets too big. Or cut him down—if he gets too powerful. The *deist* has hurled his god right out of his world—reduced him to a silent senior partner who has turned nearly everything over to man. He only hurls when God acts up—like with an earthquake, a tornado or an untimely death. The *atheist* has rationalized (another form of hurling) god right out of existence. He then spends most of his time ridiculing those who have not yet reached his conclusions. The *agnostic* is a hesitant hurler. He is not sure if God is or what God is or whether the whole thing is worthy of his critical investigation. At any rate, he postulates a god who is easy to hide from, yet it is not necessary to do so. The *liberal* hurls at God's wrath and basks in His love. The average, typical human being uses God as a crutch for moments of crisis, a catharsis for moments of confession, and a counselor for moments of confusion. The rest of the time he is a relatively respectable *theist* who conveniently sidesteps the whole issue.

Hurling is simply our way of relating—improperly and inadequately—to God. We hurl by the way we think, feel and act. By what we say or do not say. By what we do or do not do. We all do it. The pagan who says there are no absolutes is hurling at a holy God. The Christian who does not hate sin is doing the same thing. Both are undercutting God.

Because we are sinners, we hurl at everyone—even other human beings. It wasn't my fault; it was his. It wasn't my responsibility; it was hers. It isn't our problem; it is theirs. I'm not dogmatic; I'm just confident. I'm not critical; I'm just discerning. If it weren't for my husband, I'd be happy. If we could move out of this neighborhood, our problems would be solved. If I had taken this course from another professor, I could have done okay.

This is not to say that others do not have problems. Nor is it to say that we are always wrong when we blame others. It is simply to say that our tendency is to get it off our back, to shift it to someone else. Adam started it. Eve followed suit.

> 3:13 *"Then the Lord God said to the woman, 'What is this you have done?' And the woman said, 'The serpent deceived me, and I ate.'"*

God turns to the woman and confronts her with the opportunity to openly and honestly admit her guilt. You would think that Eve would have done just that. She had been standing there listening to the whole miserable dialogue her mate was having with God. She heard Adam miss choice opportunities to say the right thing. You would think she would have it all together at this point and that she would have done the right thing. But remember, Eve is now also a sinner, and she cannot help but communicate like a sinner. "It wasn't

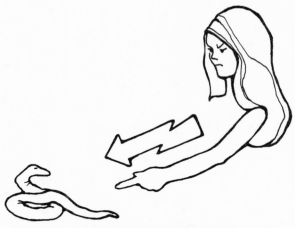

Woman Blames the Serpent

really my fault,'' she replies. ''The serpent talked me into it.''
True, but also true was the fact that she committed the act of
disobedience. She does just what Adam did. She wants to put
the blame on someone else. Everyone else had been blamed.
The serpent was the only one left. Incidentally, note that both
Adam and Eve added a brief, half-hearted admission of guilt
in the phrase ''and I ate.'' After all, nobody's perfect.

In Summary

It all started in the garden. Sin affected man's total being. Even his communication patterns were distorted by the
fall. Since then, man's tendency and temptation is to hide or
to hurl. We tend to keep things bottled up inside. We also
tend to let things out in the wrong way. In both cases we suffer the consequences—consequences within ourselves and
consequences between ourselves and others.

If the problem is related to our sinfulness, then the solution must deal with that sinfulness. That is exactly what we
are going to explore and expand in the chapters to come. But
before we do that we need to dig into the nature of the problem a bit more.

Interaction

1. How Satan communicates is an important area of study. We are not going to thoroughly treat that subject in this book, but the reader is encouraged to delve into it for himself. Some Scriptures that should be studied are: Genesis 3:1-6; Isaiah 14:12-14; Matthew 4:1-11; Luke 8:12; Acts 5:3; 2 Corinthians 4:3-4; 11:13-15; Ephesians 2:1-3; 1 John 4:4; Revelation 2:12-17; 12:9-10; 20:3.

2. Dwight Small in *Christian: Celebrate Your Sexuality* outlines the relational consequences of the fall in an interesting way (pp. 122-123). They are a worthy addition to the contents of this chapter and could be used to stimulate discussion.
   a) Man could no longer know God and understand His way. Intellectual intimacy with Him ceased.
   b) Man could no longer receive and reciprocate divine love. Emotional intimacy with God ceased.
   c) Man could no longer choose the will of God for his life. Volitional intimacy with God ceased.
   d) Man no longer had moral guidance and motivation from God. Moral intimacy with God ceased.
   e) Man no longer perceived his own intrinsic worth as deriving from God. His consciousness of self was alienated because intimacy with God ceased.
   f) Man no longer perceived his spiritual worth and destiny because his personal intimacy with God ceased.

3. We will probe this question in the next chapter, but why not think about it before you read on. Is there something inherent in the nature of sin itself that causes us to hide and hurl?

4. If you are teaching Genesis 3:7-13, why not develop a series of study questions that would stimulate the learners to personally probe these verses for their meaning and implications. Use questions that explore who, what, when, where, how and why.

5. Hiding and hurling are the two basic concepts in this chapter. Can you explain each one in your own words? Can you give examples of each from your own life?

6. "A psychologically healthy, well-educated person will have no problems communicating with others." Do you agree?

Footnotes

[1] Ephesians 2:1; Colossians 1:21; Ephesians 4:18.
[2] Romans 3:11; 1:28; 1:21, 25.
[3] Luke 18:9-14.
[4] Luke 15.
[5] Philippians 3:4-6; Romans 3:12, 20; Titus 3:15; Romans 1:18-21.
[6] Ephesians 2:2; 2 Corinthians 4:4; Jeremiah 17:9; Romans 1:25.
[7] Romans 5:8; 2 Corinthians 5:18-21.

Resources

Along with the materials suggested at the end of chapter 1, you should be aware of *Genesis 3* by Edward J. Young. Published by Banner of Truth Trust in 1966, this 164 page paperback is an excellent devotional and expository study of each of the twenty-four verses in this crucial chapter.

Jeanne Hendricks has a creative, probing chapter entitled "Three Phases of Eve" in her book, *A Woman For All Seasons,* Nelson, 1977.

Chapter 3

Self-Centered Communication

S omething is bothering me. I need to share it with my wife. But I don't. Why not?

I am upset with my teenager's behavior. I blow my stack and humiliate her in front of her friends. Why?

Somebody asks me if I am familiar with a particular concept. In all honesty I'm not, but for some strange reason I smile, nod my head up and down and mumble a half-hearted "uh-huh." Why?

Hiding and hurling is *what* we do. But *why* do we do it? Let's take a closer look.

The Root of the Problem

The essence of sin is *pride*. Pride was Satan's problem. He sought to lift himself up to be like God. Pride is *self-centeredness*. Note Satan's five self-centered "I will" statements in Isaiah 14:12-14, culminating with "I will make myself like the Most High." "Conceit" is the word used in 1 Timothy 3:6 to refer to the same incident. Satan, originally a beautiful angel, was cast out of heaven as a result of his sin. We see him later in the garden talking to Eve. He subtly tempts her to consider disobeying her Creator.

Satan appealed to Eve's innocent but latent capacity to be self-centered. She had the potential to express and experience the lust of the flesh and the lust of the eyes and boastful pride of life (1 John 2:16). She didn't have to, but she could. And she did.

Using her mind, she reasoned that the tree was good for food (the lust of the flesh), it was a delight to the eyes (the lust of the eyes), and desirable to make one wise (the pride of life). By an act of her will she took fruit from the tree and ate. Like Satan, she wanted to be like God. She followed her inclinations rather than His instructions. She then talked Adam into doing the same thing.

Prior to the fall, Adam and Eve were not conscious of good and evil, right and wrong. Having had no exposure to evil, they could have no awareness of its opposite—good. The man who has never been sick has no awareness of being *well*. That is assuming, of course, that you can isolate him from anyone else who is sick, which you can't. But Adam and Eve were totally isolated from evil. Good to them was simply that which was normal and real.

When they sinned, they immediately became aware of the reality of and distinction between good and evil. In this sense, they were now like God (Genesis 3:22). But they were also unlike God, in that they had woefully insufficient means to handle themselves as fallen people in a fallen world. Obedience to God would have been their personal commitment to a life of discipleship, i.e. putting themselves consciously and willfully under God. They chose the alternative—to exalt self. It turned out to be a miserable exaltation. A grotesque anticlimax.

Self-centered pride was Satan's problem. It was Adam and Eve's problem. Our roots go back to Adam and Eve and we have all inherited their basic sinful nature. So self-centered pride is our problem too. Yours and mine.

Self-centeredness is an active principle within us. Scripture refers to this inner, driving force as lust, desire or coveting. Paul says in Romans 7:7-8 that when the details of

Self-Centered Pride is the Problem

the law were placed alongside his instinctive human desire, it made him keenly aware of how his desires violated God's. That is what he means when he says "sin, taking opportunity through the commandment, produced in me coveting of every kind" (Romans 7:8). When you go on a stringent diet, the knowledge of what you can eat awakens an insatiable desire to have all the things you can't eat!

Deeply ingrained in each of us is the desire to operate according to the *"lust of our flesh,"* and to indulge *"the desires of the flesh and of the mind"* (Ephesians 2:3). We are *"enslaved to various lusts and pleasures"* (Titus 3:3). Because we are at heart lovers of self, the creature we worship and serve is first and foremost *ourselves* (Romans 1:25). We are programmed to focus on the big "I."

Well, you say, all these verses apply to the non-Christian. Right. But don't forget that the Christian still has the very same potential. Paul tells Christians not to *"carry out the desire of the flesh"* (Galatians 5:16). James informs the believer that he can be tempted and enticed and carried away by his own lust (James 1:14). As Christians, we have additional assets in the form of the Holy Spirit and the Word of God. These two combine to enable us to know the truth and do it.

Every human being has this deeply rooted tendency to find the focus of life in himself, to trust himself, to love himself more than others. This is what is at the root of all our problems—even our communication problems. We hide and hurl because we are proud, sinful, self-centered persons.

How Pride Hides

Look at how this actually works itself out in our own communication patterns. Pride causes me to think and act like this:

* **I Want to Be Perfect**

* **I Know I Am Not**

* **So. . .I *Hide* My Imperfections**

* **When Will I Stop Hiding?**

* **When I Am Perfect**

Let's say for example, that something is bothering me. I don't like that. It bothers me to have something bothering me! I don't enjoy carrying around an unresolved issue. I am not happy harboring the anxiety that usually goes with it. I can't concentrate. I am preoccupied. I get overly serious and moody. I pout. I don't want to be that way. I want to be a person who doesn't have things bothering him. What I would really like to be is *perfectly* unbothered.

Is that wrong? To want to be perfect in a certain area? Not categorically. But, to be legitimate, my desire for perfection must have the right goal—God's glory, not mine. The right resources—God's power, not mine. And the right time perspective—perfection is in heaven, not on earth.

I usually forget all of these criteria and function with a "do-it-for-yourself-and-by-yourself-as-soon-as-possible" philosophy. That is because I want to be perfect. I will admit that I lower my perfectionist sights now and then and aim for being reasonably and consistently super-adequate. Alas, I can't even reach that goal.

I need to realize that it is *wrong* to think I have achieved or can achieve perfection in any area in this life, but that it is *right* to want to become perfect in every area in this life, through God's power and for God's glory. Success, then, comes with every step I take in the direction of perfection. Paul saw it this way and that is why in Philippians 3 he could talk about being perfect (mature, 3:15), yet at the same time not being perfect (3:12), and thus setting his sights to move toward perfection (3:14).

I want to be perfect. I know I am not. I've been around myself long enough to know I am weak, inadequate, inconsistent. I know painfully well that there are numerous things that bother me. Sure, there are periods of time when things are just great, but they always seem to be punctuated by the unexpected, the unnecessary and the unpleasant. That's what bothers me.

I would like to live in a world that doesn't bother me. That world doesn't exist. So I struggle to become a person who won't allow anything to bother him. I am never completely successful. How well I know that!

I want to be perfect. I know I am not. So...I hide my imperfections. From whom? Well, there are a lot of things that are true about me that I either don't know about or won't admit to myself. I hide from myself. We will talk more about this later on. Right now, we are focusing on hiding from others.

Something is bothering me. One of the significant persons in my life is my wife. She has been my companion, partner and lover for over twenty-six years. Why not share it with her? Because I don't want to upset her. (Perfect people never upset anyone.) Because I don't think she could help. (But even listening helps.) Because I can handle this one on my own. (Perfect people can do it all by themselves.) Because I would rather not focus on my problems. (Perfect people aren't supposed to have them, anyway.) So for these and various other reasons I tend to hide what it is that is bothering me.

When will I stop hiding? When I am perfect. Then I will feel free to be open and honest with everyone, all the time, about anything. Because then I'll have nothing to hide. No reason to wear a mask. No need to cover up. And when, pray tell, will that happen? Never—in this life; on this earth. So I need to learn to deal with my pride and self-centeredness here and now. With God's help, I can learn how to communicate openly, honestly and appropriately with God, myself and others. But until then, pride tends to hide.

How Pride Hurls

Pride not only hides, it hurls. This is the way it works:

* **I Want Others to Be Perfect**
* **I Know They Are Not**
* **So...I *Hurl* at Their Imperfections**
* **When Will I Stop Hurling?**
* **When They Are Perfect**

I want a perfect wife. Perfect children. Perfect in-laws and grandparents. Perfect neighbors. Perfect deacons. A perfect pastor. Perfect students in my classes. Perfect associates on the faculty of the school where I work.

Proud, self-centered person that I am, I don't like to put up with ignorance, sloppiness, resistance, procrastination, inarticulateness, dishonesty, irritating habits, forgetfulness, lack of respect, discourtesy, legalism, complaining, lack of discipline, stubbornness, greed, and especially—pride and self-centeredness! I want the people that I live with and work with to be perfect—or at least not to have any faults! Why? Because it is fun and easy and pleasant to live and work with people who are okay. And I want life to be fun, easy and pleasant.

Is it wrong to want others to be perfect? No. Perfection is a legitimate goal—for me, for them. The error that creeps into our thinking is that we *expect* others to be perfect. Thus, those who are close to us don't have the right to be sinful, but they do have the responsibility of being totally sanctified! That which I demand of myself (and cannot deliver), I tend to demand of others (who cannot deliver).

I want others to be perfect. I know they are not. I live with them. I work with them. I talk with them. I watch them function. I see them miss the mark. Forget the assignment. Fail to perform adequately. React improperly. Behave immaturely. Put off indefinitely. My antennae are set up to receive perfect responses and so I scrutinize and label every response that fails to qualify. A lot of them don't. My wife isn't perfect. Nor my kids. Nor my friends.

So...I hurl at their imperfections. And I am a *creative* hurler. Sometimes I hurl myself away from them and avoid them. Robbed of my presence, they will surely see their error and change! I hurl myself at them by smothering them with positive affirmation. If I emphasize what is good, perhaps they will realize what is bad. I hurl obliquely. Avoiding direct reference to the issue, I'll weasel around with suggestions, recommendations, questions; giving them the major responsibility of properly decoding the message. I hurl angrily, lashing out with a few choice words that send the other person reeling—his shattered ego gasping for a breath of self-esteem. I hurl intellectually, seeking to impress my friend (?) with his lack of insight and my wealth of wisdom.

I hurl inconsistently. Sometimes I put up graciously with what to me is mediocrity, while at other times I'll come down hard. I hurl frontally, telling someone exactly what I think, not mincing any words, not worrying about their feelings, just telling them precisely what they need to know. I often hurl silently, internalizing the entire conversation. This gives me a chance to marshall my arguments for future external presentation. And even if I never make the external presentation, I have had the opportunity to speak my piece, and further develop my ulcer.

Is it wrong for me to be sensitive to what others are saying and doing? Wrong to evaluate their beliefs and behavior? Wrong to say something to them about what they don't know; what they aren't doing right; what they are doing wrong? Definitely not. We are to help one another grow. We cannot do this apart from evaluation and communication.

What is wrong is our tendency to communicate at the wrong time, in the wrong way, for the wrong reasons, achieving precisely the wrong results. When we do any of these things we are hurling and hurting rather than helping. The what, when, where, why and how of communication that helps is to be explored in later chapters.

When will I stop hurling? The answer is obvious. When others are perfect. When the people I live and work with get their lives together, then I'll have no reason to evaluate and criticize them. When they all say and do what they ought to, all the time, then I can accept them without qualification. When will this happen? Never—in this lifetime. So, I need to learn to deal with my imperfect family and friends here and now. And I can, with God's help, discover how to communicate openly, honestly, appropriately and effectively with others. But until then, pride tends to hurl.

In Summary

Hiding and hurling—that is my problem. I do it because I am a sinner. Being a sinner makes me essentially a self-centered person. Everything I do, including my communication, tends to revolve around myself. What is it I want for myself? The best. Nothing but the best. I want the best *in* myself. I want to be a perfect person. I want the best *for* myself. I want to have perfect friends. Ironic, isn't it, that the very thing that makes us expect perfection in ourselves and others keeps us from achieving it. We are wretchedly complex persons. We need help. In Christ it is available.

Interaction

1. What examples of hiding and/or hurling do you find in the following passages of Scripture?
   Genesis 4:1-8
   Genesis 12:10-20
   Genesis 20:1-18

2. Analyze Peter's words in Matthew 16:22. Could they be classified as hurling? Do you see anything in the context that would cause us to identify pride as the reason for these words? Would you classify Christ's response in verse twenty-three as hurling?

3. Here are some questions that will help you explore the concepts presented in this chapter. They could profitably be discussed in small groups.
   * What do I tend to hide?
   * From whom do I tend to hide?
   * What happens when I hide?
   * When do I tend to hurl?
   * At whom do I tend to hurl?
   * What happens when I hurl?

4. Can you think of any situations where pride has caused you to hide and/or hurl in the past few days?

Resources

This chapter deals with egotism and its implications for our communication patterns. One of the best resources on self-centeredness is the *The God-Players* by Earl Jabay, Zondervan Publishing House, 1969. In it you will find a stimulating presentation of both the problem and solution of pride.

Chapter 4

How We Hide and Hurl

Meet some friends of mine. Actually, you will find that you already know most of these folks. Maybe not by the same names, but you will recognize them by what they say or don't say. As a matter of fact, you'll probably feel like you're meeting yourself here and there in this chapter.

So come along with me as we verbally and visually develop some brief case studies that illustrate certain kinds of hiding and hurling patterns. You will get more out of each situation, if, after you have interacted with the concept, you will pause and think through when, where, how and why you tend to do that very same thing or something similar. Many of the illustrations given relate to marriage, because this is a major area of communication. Fill in, in your own mind, some of the other relationships which could also be pictured.

We Tend to Hide Negative and Positive

We get so used to keeping to ourselves those thoughts and feelings that would be considered negative that we tend to hide a lot of other things—even those thoughts and feelings that would be considered positive. The result—our communication pattern dwindles down to that which is neither plus or minus, but neutral.

Here is Silent Sam. He seldom complains. He seldom compliments. Excitement? Depression? He shows little of either. He is not sarcastic. Nor is he very affectionate. He is just nice—and neutral. When asked what happened today at work, he summarizes eight hours of human drama with all of its problems and pressures, victories and defeats, challenges and insights, with a cryptic "Nothing." His wife's new dress is "OK." Tomorrow's plans are "Whatever you say." What it is that is bothering him is "Nothing important." When asked to share it he "would rather not talk about it." Silent Sam. Or Silent Sally. The shell is well-constructed and neatly wrapped around them. All we really see and hear is Surface Sam, not the real Sam. He features himself as the strong, silent type. But strength is not always synonymous with silence. Granted, we are to be quick to hear and slow to speak (James 1:19). True, we are to be careful about multiplying words when a simple Yes or No would suffice (Matthew 5:37). But, at the same time, we are obligated to speak the truth (Ephesians 4:15, 25), and the truth includes that which is causing Sam to suffer and to rejoice (1 Corinthians 12:26). The ultimate goal of our words is to edify (Ephesians 4:29). Sam's communication pattern keeps people *guessing*. God wants us to communicate in such a way that we keep ourselves and our relationships with others *growing*.

That Which We Hide—May Evaporate

Meet Sensitive Steve. He is returning from his morning coffee break with some unexpected, unwelcome news. The company is thinking of replacing Steve with a computer. That is bad news. Steve doesn't say anything; he just mulls it over for the rest of the day. He can't dismiss it from his mind, so he has to deal with it. By noon he has processed the problem to the point where it doesn't seem nearly as big and bad. By 5:00 he has it essentially resolved in his own mind.

Steve handled this issue in a few hours. Sometimes, because of differences in personality and/or more difficult problems, it takes longer—a few days, even weeks. But keeping things to ourselves isn't always bad. It may be the mature way to handle things. I say "mature" because what we do when we keep it to ourselves can be very biblical. It is called *meditation.*

The "meditations of our heart" are to be acceptable in God's sight (Psalm 19:14). With minds renewed by the Word of God we are able to engage in this kind of mature meditation (Psalm 1:2; Ephesians 4:23). That is what Steve is doing—meditating maturely. He is undoubtedly communicating the truth of Romans 8:28 to the situation. God, not the company, is in ultimate control of his life. That doesn't make the problem evaporate, but it certainly helps to put it into the proper perspective.

Some issues are so fleeting and insignificant that we can mull them over quickly and they soon disappear. Others take more time and more thought to effectively process, but eventually, as we develop the proper perspective they too will fade from our inner agenda. Thank God for the ability to think things through and forget. Paul indicates in Philippians 3:13 that one major aspect of his philosophy of life was to forget the past and concentrate on becoming a future, goal-oriented person. He knew how to meditate maturely.

That Which We Hide—May Ferment

Fermentation is the process of active and often disorderly development. Some of the things we hide don't fade away, they stay right there and ferment. As they ferment, they expand and envelop us. Sometimes there is an explosion.

Gloomy Gloria is a single young adult who just got through looking at her friend's new diamond and hearing all about the wedding plans. Glenda wants to marry, but right now she hardly even dates. In scene one she is processing this data.

Scene two. Now she is looking in the mirror—at the skin blemishes, the stringy hair, the funny shaped nose—and concludes that she is not very attractive and will probably never marry. Feeding on such distraught data, the fermentation process continues.

Scene three. Sitting alone in her apartment she is thinking: "I am doomed to celibacy. Nobody really likes me. I am a failure. I will never be happy." Glenda is not meditating with God. She is commiserating with herself. She is not gaining perspective; she is losing it. As someone has aptly said: "When you have yourself for a doctor, you have a fool for a patient.'' She needs to tell herself what God thinks about her and the nature of His plan for her life.

That is often the way of life for us. Problems attack us, invade us and then proceed to occupy larger and larger areas of our mental and emotional territory. Many issues we choose to hide refuse to lie dormant; they roar and roam around and claw at our soul. That is what can happen when we harbor unconfessed sin. It infiltrates every nook and cranny of our lives. David kept a certain sin unresolved for a long while and during that time he was miserable (Psalm 32:3-4).

Anger, if not processed quickly and completely, can go through the same fermentation process, resulting in all kinds of internal and external problems. Scripture wisely instructs us not to let the sun go down on our anger (Eph. 4:26).

Let me introduce you to Irate Ira. He is even-tempered...always mad. Well, not always, but he is right now.

· Irate Ira ·

In scene one he is pretty peeved about the neighbor's kids and their dog. In the next scene he is really stewing. Carrying on "militant meditation"! In the final scene he loses what little cool he has left, comes unglued and explodes. In more ways than one, Ira has blown it! This drama may have taken just a few minutes, or it may have taken a few months.

Imperfect neighbors don't have perfect kids or dogs. Their dogs don't bark perfectly. Their kids don't act perfectly. Ira needs to remind himself of this. One of the fruits of the Spirit is patience. Another is longsuffering. Kindness. Gentleness. And—dare we mention it—self-control. Ira needs to meditate on these things.

Hiding is tricky business. Some issues evaporate. Others tend to ferment. Processing the data with a Word-oriented meditation is the best way to facilitate the evaporation process and to neutralize dangerous fermentation.

The More We Hide—The Less We Share

Hiding often causes us to "interiorize" the communication process. That is, we talk to ourselves a lot. This is not wrong, except that it does have a tendency to make us more closed and isolated persons.

This is Mac Muller. He thinks a lot. With and to himself. He doesn't share much of his thinking with others. The

longer he carries on his internal dialogue, the less he tends to open up to his family and friends. We call him shy, quiet, reserved, withdrawn, introspective, etc. He will question his motives. "Why did I ever do that?" He queries the attitudes and actions of others. "Wonder what he meant by saying that?" "Why didn't she do what she promised?" He frequently carries on internal courtroom scenes—presenting his carefully articulated arguments for the prosecution and the defense; playing the roles of both, plus acting as judge and jury. In his mind he replays recent incidents from his own experience; emphasizing the pleasant aspects of the scene and determining what he could have said or done that would have been better. Mac is working toward his masters degree in mulling.

However, the person who internalizes so much tends to wrap a thicker shell around himself and communicate less of real significance to others. We get used to talking to ourselves. It is comfortable, non-threatening and non-demanding. To engage in similar conversations with others— to reveal to them what we are thinking and feeling and why— puts the kind of stress on us that causes us to stay in our own self-enclosed auditorium.

The answer is not to think less and talk more! The answer is to learn to communicate openly, honestly and appropriately the essence of what I am thinking and feeling— communicate it *to myself and to others*. The New Testament knows nothing of an isolated lifestyle. We are to assemble together and encourage and stimulate one another (Hebrews 10:24-25). We are to regard ourselves as interdependent members of a body and as such we are to communicate the things that are causing us to suffer or rejoice (1 Corinthians 12:25-26).

The more we keep it in; the harder it is to let it out. Internal mulling is not the best way to learn to communicate with others. The best way to learn to communicate with others is to communicate with others!

The More We Keep In—The Less We Let In

The shell that keeps us from exposing ourselves also serves to protect us from invasion. Here is Mac once again.

See how the tendency to bottle things up within also causes him to barricade himself from those without. His wife is probably saying something like this: "Mac and I have really been struggling with some problems in our relationship with his parents. But he is so stingy with words. He just doesn't want to talk about it. When I express my thoughts and feelings to him, I get no response. He won't listen to me. I can't seem to get through to him." Mac's children and his business associates would probably echo the same appraisal. He is hard to get through to.

Often those who don't talk much, don't listen well. They listen to themselves, but they easily tune out others. They don't readily take the risk of verbally venturing very far outside their shell, nor do they allow others to semantically intrude inside the shell. Hiding has side effects. Among other things, it makes us hard to talk to.

When We Hurl—We Usually Hurt Others

How do you react when comments like these are directed at you?

"Shut up and listen to me."

"Can't you do anything right?"

"Late again, huh?"

"Who do you think you are, anyway?"

"That was a dumb thing to do."

"Go away and leave me alone."

"You need to shape up."

"Why don't you watch where you are going?"

"I told you it wouldn't work."

When you are on the receiving end of such remarks, you feel bad. They hurt. Sometimes they are deliberately designed to hurt. They are hurled because someone is mad at you; wants to get even with you. At other times they aren't directed specifically at you and may not even be communicated with the intention of hurting—but you get caught in the crossfire, you get hit, and you feel pain. Then there are times when the statement seems harmless, but just beneath the surface is a militant message.

"I failed to make myself clear." (You weren't listening.)

"Are you saying...?" (You don't know what you are talking about.)

"I misunderstood you." (You are hopelessly muddled.)

"Well, I see that time is running out." (You have taken up another meeting with your yapping. We will have to call another session.)

Admittedly, these are tongue-in-cheek translations, but the point is that there are times when hurling is partially hidden behind some typical cliches.

Words can hurt. Absolutes like "always" and "never" have very sharp points. "You never do anything right." "You never pick up your clothes." "You never discipline the children." "You never clean up the garage." "You always come home late." "You always forget to empty the garbage." "You always put your interests first."

Using "never" and "always" with regard to someone's behavior is classifying them as the epitome of imperfection. Telling them they are consistently bad. That hurts!

When we hurl we may hit our mate, our children, our parents, brothers and sisters, the dog or cat, a post, the automobile accelerator, a fellow employee, a customer, or even an innocent bystander. We also hurl non-verbally with the look on our face, the nod of our head, and the shrug of our shoulders. When she got mad as a toddler, one of our girls used to sit down in the middle of the room, take off one shoe and throw it, then take off her sock, wad it up and throw it, and then repeat the process with the other shoe and sock. Adults are more sophisticated hurlers. We wad up well-chosen words and throw them. On second thought, I'm not so sure. A young wife told me that when her husband got mad, he hurled a few choice words at her, then hurled his tools all over the garage, then got in the car and hurled it down the nearest freeway!

The Bible says we are all to cull the unwholesome words out of our conversation (Ephesians 4:29). They are described in the context as lying, bitterness, wrath, anger, clamor, slander and malice (4:25, 26, 31). That rules out hurling and hurting. Such words do not only hurt other human beings, but they also grieve the Holy Spirit (4:30). Instead, we are to use words that are gracious, kind, come from a tender heart and evidence a forgiving—rather than a retaliating—spirit (4:29, 32).

When we have been Hit and Hurt— We Tend to Hurl back, then Withdraw and Hide

"You never listen to what I am saying!"

"That's because you never say anything worth listening to!"

When someone has wounded us with words, our natural tendency is to fire a semantic salvo right back at them. The response of a wounded ego is retaliation. Get even. The quickest way to accomplish this is with words aimed directly at our adversary's ego.

Hurl, then Hide

Once we get even—we get out of range. It is no fun to get hurt. To avoid it we withdraw to a safe place where the other person can't hit us and hurt us. We gradually retreat away and hide from any kind of meaningful relationship with the person. We retreat by not talking at all; and finally by going our separate ways. Couples can live in the same house and deacons can serve on the same board yet be involved in one of the first two phases of withdrawal.

But Christians, regardless of how sensitive and sore we may be from previous word battles, are obligated to continue speaking the truth in love (Ephesians 4:15, 25); to work at being of one mind on issues (Philippians 2:2); and to develop a forebearing spirit (Ephesians 4:2). That last concept—forebearing—is an instructive one. It means to tolerate or to put up with. The Lord used it when He talked about having to "put up with" the unbelief of Israel (Mark 9:19).

Scripture realistically faces the fact that when imperfect people live and work together they must learn to put up with one another. To tolerate the differences and disagreements that will invariably occur. In Colossians 3:12-13 Paul surrounds this concept of "bearing with one another" with two important components. The last word in verse 12 is "patience." This means to withhold anger and to be long suffering (cf. 2 Peter 3:9 *"The Lord...is patient toward you"*). Here is one important dimension of learning to put up with one another: don't retaliate! The other dimension is found in the phrase that follows: "forgiving each other." Instead of retaliating, retreating, pouting and nursing your bruised ego into a full-fledged grudge—forgive! That is precisely the way in which God relates to us (3:13b). How can we do any less when relating to others? How can we embrace this truth and live at arm's length from one another? Paul expressed his philosophy of relationships like this:

when we are reviled, we bless;

when we are persecuted, we endure;

when we are slandered, we try to conciliate (1 Corinthians 4:12-13).

The More We Hide and Hurl—
The More We Isolate Ourselves

The more we hide things within ourselves, the more we withdraw from others. The more we hurl things, the more others withdraw from us. Hiding and hurling contribute to alienation.

The wall that stands between us was built by both of us. Each one contributed bricks and mortar. It isn't solid, there is an open space here and there where we can still communicate about certain things and at certain times. We may use some glass brick, so we can at least see, if not hear, one another. And some fire brick—to withstand some of our more caustic comments.

Continued Hurling and Hiding Builds a Separating Wall

The existence of the wall is frustating to us. We want to get rid of it. We have trouble deciding which bricks are mine; which are yours. It is a slow, tedious, sometimes traumatic process. We want to find that one brick, which when pulled out, will cause the entire wall to collapse. We cannot find it. We must take this wall down just like we built it. Brick by brick. We find it difficult to dispose of the bricks. We keep a few choice ones piled up nearby. We might need them for a constructive argument.

We may have trouble getting started on the wall. Or we may get stalled along the way. A third party can help. A competent counselor is what we need. This is not a sign of weakness. It is a sign of strength. One dimension of maturity is knowing what we cannot do and asking someone who can help us. Don't expect him to blow his trumpet and make the wall instantly collapse. He will help us determine who put which bricks where and why. We still have to remove them. Brick by brick. It takes work to be at peace with all men. It is worthwhile work.

Temporary Relief can come by Sharing the Common Ground we Still Have

A weekend at the coast. A week in the mountains. A day at Disneyland. Supper at the steakhouse. An evening with special friends. We can always find ways of submerging our differences and distances and have a good time together.

Sharing Common Ground is a Temporary Solution

Even though Tom and Linda are spending a beautiful afternoon at the beach and are relating obviously well on the common ground they have between them, there are still some very definite unresolved issues in their relationship. This time on the beach may contribute very little to the ultimate resolution of their problem.

This is the illusion we labor under. That we can go away from our battleground and when we return the war will be over. Not so. That we can remodel and refurnish the house and then we will be able to live peacefully together. Not so. That we can make love to one another and the ecstasy of that shared experience will break down all the other barriers. Not so. That we can buy gifts, pay compliments, make minor concessions, rearrange furniture, switch to the day shift, have children, take vacations, give up a habit, move across town, get another job, go back to school, admit we were wrong, and on and on—do one or any number of these things and our relationship will be all that we desire it to be. Not so. That we can attend church and sit together and worship together and serve together and as a result we will have fellowship with one another. Not so.

There are no shortcuts to the development and maintaining of unity and harmony. No quick, simple ways to bring down the wall between us. Even Christians, in whom God is at work, must cooperate with God and each other to work out their interpersonal relationships (Philippians 2:12-13).

We Tend to Communicate Selectively

We can be nice to our secretary and mean to our wife. All in one day. I can show concern for one student and contempt for another. In the same class hour. A man may share little or nothing with his wife and family but pour his heart out to the bartender, a buddy at work, or his pastor. The point is that we are selective in our communication patterns. We don't hurl at *everyone*. We don't hurl at anyone *all the time*. We don't hide from *everyone*. Nor do we hide *all the time* from anyone. We hide from certain people. In certain kinds of situations. We hurl at certain people. In certain kinds of circumstances.

When I am fatigued and under pressure to get something done, I can hurl at anyone who gets near. When I am depressed and worried about something, I can hide, regardless of whom I am with.

Look at Henrietta. At breakfast she gives her husband a few solid linguistic licks. At the women's Bible study later that morning she gently edifies Edna. At the supermarket at noon, she chides the checkout boy for failing to remember the noodles were on sale. She pauses at midafternoon to visit a sick friend and cheers her up with words of comfort and encouragement. She picks up Harold, Jr., from kindergarten, buys him an ice cream cone, and then gives him a vocabulary lesson when he proceeds to drip it all over the front seat. And during the day there were numerous times when she wanted and needed to share some of her inner thoughts and feelings, but she kept them hidden. She wore her mask all day. Is Henrietta schizophrenic? No—just imperfect! What does she need? What all of us need. Someone who can help us deal with our communication problem—our tendency to hide and hurl. Someone who can enable us to share—openly, honestly and appropriately.

In Summary

You have undoubtedly identified personally with some of the foregoing illustrations and aptly applied some of them to others you know. The point is that we are complex, creative communicators. We hide and hurl in a variety of ways. The problem is a complicated one. So complicated that we need insight from a master communicator. We shall explore that possibility in the next chapter.

Interaction

1. Like Sensitive Steve, what are some of the things that you find easy to adequately process?

2. Like Gloomy Glenda, what are some of the issues in your life that tend to ferment?

3. What makes you act like Irate Ira?

4. John and Martha have built a wall between them. Only one of them is seeing a counselor about the problem. Will this help?

5. Which do you tend to do more—hide or hurl? Why?

6. One way to get people to interact with the contents of this chapter would be to make overhead transparencies of one or more of the scenes. As you project each one on the screen, have the group discuss what could be happening and why. You could also ask them what biblical principles·could be applied in each situation.

Resources

1. For insight on the whole process of dialogue, with a good discussion of the barriers to communication: *The Miracle of Dialogue* by Reuel L. Howe, The Seabury Press, 1963.

2. For a creative treatment of marital communication: *Communication: Key to Your Marriage* by H. Norman Wright, Regal Books, 1974.

Part 2
Developing the Solution

Chapter 5

The Master Communicator

I had been counseling with Bob for a number of weeks. "Bob," I said, "I'm leaving this Friday for a three week vacation." He got a worried look on his face and said, "Who am I going to talk to while you are gone?"

That was the turning point for Bob. He began to realize that I wasn't the only one he could talk with. My leaving caused him to take some painful but positive steps of personal growth.

But it was a turning point for me too. Bob's words prompted me to blurt out to him, "Wait a minute. Even though I am leaving, there is someone else you can talk to. Someone who never takes a vacation—God!"

I then realized that I had been so intent on providing counsel for Bob that I had failed to develop his communication with God. At that point I began more seriously than ever before to explore this business of having real communication with God. Let's explore it together in this chapter.

The Need Stated

An adequate solution to our communication problems will have to deal with the following needs:

1. **I Need a Relationship with a Person** *From Whom I Cannot Hide.*

2. **I Need a Relationship with a Person** *At Whom I Can Hurl* **but who Gives Me No Cause To and Won't Be Alienated If I Do.**

3. **I Need a Relationship with a Person** *Who Will Always Tell Me The Truth.*

In short, I need a friend who knows me completely, at whom I can holler without offending, and who will always tell me exactly what I need to know. These criteria rule out all my friends! I can hide from them. I can hide from my working associates, from my students, from my pastor, from my children and even from my wife, who knows me better than anyone else. I can also hurl at any of these people, but eventually I will alienate them by my hurling. Futhermore, none of my friends will always tell me only the truth. They will mix in their opinions and prejudices as well as outright error.

Only God can meet my Needs

Only one person meets all of the necessary require-ments—and that person is GOD.

The preceding diagram visually depicts the problem and the solution. On the horizontal plane, among all of my human relations, no one qualifies to meet my communication needs and solve my communication problem. But there is another dimension, the vertical, which brings a divine person, God, into the picture. I must bring Him into the situation because He alone is fully qualified to meet my communica-tion needs and solve my communication problem.

I cannot hide from God. He is always with me. He knows me intimately and completely. I can hurl at God, if necessary, but He gives me no cause to and He won't be alienated if I do. I can and will receive from God, only and always, the truth. If God is the one and only person before whom I am transparent, with whom I can share anything, and from whom the truth comes, *then I need a relationship with God.* Christianity offers me this relationship with God—the Master Communicator!

Salvation	gives me a relationship with God wherein I am completely and continually ac-cepted because of my position in Christ.
Sanctification	allows me to develop this relationship with God by listening to Him in His Word and by talking to Him in prayer.

Salvation and Communication

Salvation *involves* communication. God communicates good news to man. The gospel is a set of carefully selected words about the sin of man, the death of Christ and the resur-rection of Christ (1 Corinthians 15:1-8). People need to hear these words (Romans 10:17), and communicate their accept-ing response to God. This response is described with such terms as confess, call, believe, obey, and receive.[1] At the heart of salvation is communication, for the gospel is a revelation from God which demands a response from man.

Salvation *insures* communication. When man responds positively to the good news, he is given what he needs—a relationship with God. Because of his new position in Christ—he is completely and continually accepted by God—he is at peace with God.[2] This insures the reality of communication with God. As a member of the family he can communicate with the heavenly Father. He can talk with God anytime, anywhere, under any circumstances, and he can say anything. Nothing the believer can say will sever his relationship with God.

I mentioned this to a group and a young woman told me afterward that she had always been very careful with her prayers, because she had been taught that if she said the wrong thing, God would disown her! Words are powerful. Potent enough to sever relationships with other people. But the believer does not have in his vocabulary words potent enough to separate him from God (cf. Romans 8:35-39).

Salvation is not a flimsy, flippant relationship with a capricious God who easily gets miffed and disowns a child who says the wrong thing. For the true believer there are no unpardonable words. Salvation is a deep, personal, permanent relationship between the individual and God. It comes into being as the result of the process of communication. It insures a circuit that is always open between us and God. It cannot be terminated by anything we say.

Second Timothy 2:12-13 appears to contradict the above statements. It says: *"If we deny Him, He also will deny us; If we are faithless, He remains faithful; for He cannot deny Himself"* (cf. Matthew 10:32-33). I believe the best way to interpret this and still remain true to the teaching of the Word with regard to the eternally secure position of the believer in Christ, is to view it as a reference to one who is not saved. He denies Christ. Christ must deny him. He is faithless. Christ remains faithful to His character; He cannot deny His holiness and justice. On the other hand, a believer can deny the Lord and still remain a believer. Peter did it (Matthew 26:69-75).

Sanctification and Communication

Vertical implications. In salvation the lines of communication are *opened* between God and man. We are put on speaking terms with God. In the process of sanctification the lines of communication are *operating* between God and man. In simplistic terms, communication is speaking and listening. Sanctification involves these same two components. In the Scriptures God tells us what we need to know in order to grow. The process of growth, or sanctification, thus demands that we *listen* to what God has to say to us. The Word that effects our spiritual birth (1 Peter 1:23) is the same Word that causes our spiritual growth (1 Peter 2:2). In sanctification we not only listen to God, we also *talk* to Him, in prayer. The prayer of faith that saves becomes the foundation for the continuing conversation with God. This is a very brief, simple analysis of sanctification. But it is a basic one. Sanctification and communication are inextricably related to each other. When there is no communication with God, there can be no real, biblical sanctification. When there is real, genuine communication to and from God, there will be real, biblical sanctification.

When we use the word "sanctification," we are using it in the same sense that Paul uses the word in 1 Thessalonians 4:3. In that passage, the apostle tells the church at Thessalonica that the will of God for their lives is their sanctification. Sanctification means *holy*, and that which is holy is separated from sin and set apart to God. Verse 1 of that chapter tells us that this kind of holy living is pleasing to God.

Edification, growth and maturity are terms the Scripture also uses to describe the process of sanctification. We can define it as the process of depending on the Spirit of God to know the Word of God and do the will of God in order to become more and more like the Son of God. That entire process involves the establishing and developing of communication between myself and God. The following diagram depicts what we are saying:

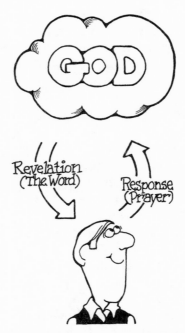

Sanctification and Communication: Vertical

God reveals saving truth to man. Man hears it, understands it, and responds to it with a personal "I believe." Then God continues to reveal sanctifying truth to the believer, who hears it, understands it, and responds to it. The essence of Christianity is revelation and response.

Horizontal implications. Sanctification, however, is not simply a person-to-God experience. It also, at the same time, has horizontal, person-to-person implications. My relationship to God will affect my relations with myself and with others. The Lord welded all of these relationships together when He said, *"You shall love the Lord your God. . .and. . . you shall love your neighbor as yourself"* (Matthew 22:37). In this passage the Christian's basic relationships (to God, self and neighbor) are outlined, and the Christian's basic responsibility (to love) is presented. We can show our relationships and responsibility in this way:

Sanctification and Communication: Horizontal

We love God by keeping His commandents (John 14:15). One of His basic commandments is for us to *listen* to Him as He speaks to us in His Word. Another is for us to *talk* to Him in prayer. So we love God by engaging in a communication process with Him. As we do this we will be growing in our ability to love our neighbor as ourself. How do I love my neighbor? By acting to meet his needs (1 John 3:17-18). John says a spoken word is not satisfactory when the neighbor's need requires a deed (v. 18). But the Scriptures in general emphasize the fact that *good words* are an essential ingredient in our *good works*. James, for example, has much to say about the believer's use and abuse of words in relationships with others. He deals with anger, partiality, teaching, quarrels, judging, arrogance, complaining, swearing, and confession.[3] This epistle, which strongly supports the importance of a faith that produces works (2:14-26), underscores the fact that our words are a significant and strategic aspect of our works.

As I am developing my communication relationship with God, I will be developing my communication relationships with myself and others. As the process of sanctification is taking place, I ought to be communicating more effectively with myself and with others—listening more effectively; talking more effectively. This ties the vertical and the horizontal

Sanctification OR Interpersonal Relationships

together. There is a very real sense in which theology is interpersonal.

The illustration on the left emphasizes the process of sanctification as it involves the individual in relationship with God. The illustration on the right shows the same person in relationship to another individual. Now, what we can and often do, is not to link sanctification (vertical) and interpersonal relationships (horizontal). We are always interested in both, but we have to go beyond interest to *integration*. If we don't integrate, we can easily work on having loving, effective relationships with others on the basis of developing a pleasing personality and mastering human relations skills. This can be done apart from God, but what we are saying is that sanctification should produce among other things—a pleasing personality and effective human relation skills!

So, why not visualize it in this manner:

Sanctification AND Interpersonal Relationships

Now we view the person in relation to God and to others at the same time. This helps integrate human and divine relationships. It also helps us realize the interdependency of these relationships. Let's carry the illustration one step further. We can't relate God to ourselves and isolate Him from others. In one way or another He is involved in every person's life. Others may not be communicating with Him, but He is still involved in their lives. We can show it in this way:

Sanctification WITH Interpersonal Relationships

I am in relationship with God. At the same time I am in relationships with others—family members, neighbors, fellow-Christians in the local church, business associates, school friends, etc. All of these relationships can be viewed in a communications framework. Let me supply some of the functions of this framework. Trace each function on the diagram.

I am learning to *listen* to God. I am listening to learn from God. This orients me to listen carefully and constructively to others. I listen in order to learn from God through them. I also listen in order to learn more about them so as to be able to more effectively share His truth with them.

I am also learning to *talk* to God about those things that are significant about me; significant about Him; and significant in our relationship. I am learning to talk to God openly, honestly, appropriately and trustfully. This orients me in talking with others. I talk to them about those things that are significant in my life; significant in their lives; and significant in our relationship. I do this openly, honestly, appropriately and trustfully.

Because I am saved and being sanctified, I have the privilege and responsibility of communicating with God. Because I am a living human being with all the elements of personality I have the privilege and responsibility of communicating with myself and with other human beings. Note, then, that the person who is in touch with God, myself and others is ME! I am a strategic factor in the communication process. I must know how to communicate. I must be an effective, articulate speaker. An interested, responsive listener. An open, authentic person. I can become this kind of a communicator because I am involved in an ongoing communication relationship with God—the Master Communicator. In subsequent chapters we are going to explore the nature of this God-man communication process and see how it can affect our *intra*personal and *inter*personal communication.

The Secular Solution

We have shown that there is a communication problem in our world and that a relationship with God is crucial to the solution. The secular world also recognizes that a problem exists.

Let's take a closer look at Tom and Linda in chapter 4. When we left them, they had built a separating wall between them, a result of their continual hurling and hiding. How do they go about solving their problem?

Their first approach will probably be to use all of their own insights and abilities to open the clogged lines of communication. If they are mature, and work at it diligently, they may be able to repair the relationship. If not, then one or both of them will probably seek help. Help comes in many forms today. A friend, a family member, a pastor, a professionally trained counselor, a good book, Ann Landers, a seminar or conference, etc. Let us call this outside resource, whatever form it takes, a counselor, and put it into the diagram thusly:

Counselors can Mediate and Help...

A counselor can be very effective in helping people who are hiding and hurling at each other. But he has limitations. He does not have X-ray perception. Counselees can hide from him. He is not perfect. Counselees may hurl at him. Even become alienated from him. The counselor also has his own tendencies to hide and hurl. He may be doing this currently in other relationships, which can affect his counseling. He may even be doing it with the counselees. Finally, the counselor doesn't have complete insight into human problems nor full wisdom about solutions.

Having tried it on their own, and having sought counsel, the couple has essentially availed themselves of the basic resources and insight which the world has to offer. That's all an unsaved couple can do. And what would a Christian couple do? Probably the very same thing. Try to work it out on their own. If that was not successful, consult a third party.

Then what is the difference between a Christian and a non-Christian approach to this? The difference is that the Christian can and should add the divine dimension to the whole process. He does not necessarily go through a different process, he simply adds God's wisdom and God's power to the normal process.

...but God's Wisdom and Power makes the Difference

The Christian Solution

If one or both of the couple have a growing relationship with God, they have access to some quality insights about their problem and how to solve it. Some of these insights will be in addition to what the world offers; some will be corrective to what the world offers; and some will reinforce what the world offers. The indwelling Holy Spirit will enable them to understand and apply these insights to their particular situation.

If they go to a Christian counselor who has a growing relationship with God, they may receive some or much of this God-oriented insight from the counselor. If they go to a non-Christian counselor they have the capacity to evaluate his counsel on the basis of their growing relationship to God. Many Christians don't have this kind of insightful relationship with God and should, if at all possible, seek the help of Christian counselors.

The secular world leaves God out of the picture and is essentially shut up to the secular human relations expert to facilitate good communication. This does not mean that all secular communication is doomed to failure nor that secular communication principles are wrong. Those who have no relationship with God can still discover and use communication principles that are in harmony with God. What it does mean is that a significant relationship that bears on man's communication problem and its solution is missing. The Christian has this relationship. A relationship with a Person from whom he cannot hide; at whom he can hurl, but has no reason to and won't be cut off if he does; and a Person who will always tell him the truth. In Christ we can have this relationship with God—the Master Communicator.

Interaction

1. *Why* do I need a relationship with a person from whom I cannot hide?

   Why do I need a relationship with a person at whom I can hurl?

   Why do I need a relationship with a person who will always tell me the truth?

2. Only God fully meets the three needs outlined at the beginning of this chapter. But to what extent are parents to meet these needs for their child? A husband and wife for each other? A pastor for his people? A teacher for his students?

3. "You can be getting along well with God and poorly with others at the same time." In the light of this chapter, how would you react to this statement?

4. In what ways can sanctification be viewed as a communication process?

5. "Mature Christian couples should be able to work out their problems without the help of a counselor." Discuss.

6. In teaching this chapter make sure your people understand our three communication needs; help them explore the fact that no other human being can adequately meet these needs; and guide them into the concept that only God can and will meet these needs.

Footnotes

[1] Romans 10:8-17; John 1:12; Acts 6:7.
[2] Romans 5:1; John 5:24; 2 Corinthians 5:17-21.
[3] James 1:19-20; 2:1-9; 3:1ff; 4:1-2, 11-12, 16; 5:9, 12, 16; See also 1:26; 2:12; 3:1-18.

Resources

1. For insight on counseling: *Effective Biblical Counseling* by Lawrence J. Crabb, Jr., Zondervan, 1977; *Dying to Live* by Bob Smith, Word Books, 1976.

2. For insight on the interpersonal implications of salvation and sanctification: *God's Forgetful Pilgrims* by Michael Griffiths, Eerdmans, 1975.

Chapter 6

Listening to God

*N*o doubt about it. He speaks to Himself. He speaks to angels. He speaks to Satan. He speaks to man. God communicates—not only for dialogue, but also for disclosure. He makes Himself known through creation. He reveals more intimate details about Himself through His Son, Jesus Christ—the living Word. He articulates all truth man needs to know in the Scriptures—the written Word. God is a communicator![1]

God's Communication Process

God is the source—the sender. He encodes and transmits the message. That message has been sovereignly preserved for us in the Bible. Man receives and decodes the message. The process of receiving and decoding involves feedback, wherein man verbalizes what he hears and understands—to himself, to others and to God. God's ultimate goal is that man comprehends the message, conforms to its truth, and communicates it to others. In this chapter we want to investigate *how* God communicates to us. We are going to extract from the Scriptures a series of communication principles.

First, we will examine the communication principle itself and determine what it teaches us about God as a communicator. This will enable us to focus on the believer and explore how he should listen to God. The diagram below shows what we have in mind.

God Speaks to Me

This shows what takes place when I am personally and privately involved in listening to God, that is, when I am reading, studying and meditating in the Scriptures on my own, by myself. This calls for competent listening on my part. The more I know about how God speaks to me, the better equipped I can be to listen to Him. We will be commenting along the way on how we can sharpen Bible study (listening) skills.

More often than not, God uses the medium of another person(s) to communicate His message to us. It may be a preacher, a teacher, the writer of a book or article, a film maker, an actor, a singer, a Bible study group leader, a person on radio, television or cassette tape. He is a multi-media communicator! Communication mediated through others to us can be visualized in this way.

God Speaks to Me through Others

Do you see the obvious conclusion? We must develop our skills in listening to others—because God communicates His Word to us through others.

God not only speaks *to* us *through* others, He also speaks *through* us *to* others. Sometimes we receive truth *from* others. At other times we transmit truth *to* others. Knowing how God communicates His truth to us helps us know how to communicate His truth to others. This dimension of the process can be visualized in this manner:

God Speaks through Me to Others

So what we intend to do in this chapter is explore each communication principle in terms of the following questions:

1. What does it tell us about how God communicates to us?

2. What does this mean in terms of my *listening to God.*

3. What does this mean in terms of my *listening to others?*

4. What does this mean in terms of my *talking to others?*

Principle #1—God's Communication Involves the Holy Spirit

God is the author of the "team teaching" concept. There are three on this team—Father, Son and Spirit. They are all equally and supremely qualified to communicate truth. They all have (self-granted!) tenure. At this stage in God's program the Holy Spirit is the resident teacher. Resident, because He *resides* in every believer.[2] He gives us truth, for He is the Spirit of truth.[3] We have what we need—a relationship with a person who will always tell us the truth.

How does He go about this? Not as a cold, impersonal commentator, but as a warm, friendly companion who comes alongside as our helper.[4] He teaches and reminds us; He bears witness to us; He guides, speaks and discloses all the truth to us.[5] His ultimate purpose in communicating truth is simple and singular—to glorify Christ.[6]

What does this mean in terms of my *listening to God?* First, I must be rightly related to this divine Teacher who indwells me. This is a relationship wherein I believe He is present and consciously depend on Him for insight and ability. Two key phrases that refer to this process are "be filled with the Spirit" and "walk by the Spirit."[7] Second, I must recognize that the Spirit communicates the Word of God.[8] If the Spirit is to speak to me, I must expose myself to the Word. Third, the Spirit is resident *within* me. He is an internal Teacher. My tendency is to wear a mask and hide behind it. He is behind that mask, talking to the real, inner me.

What does this mean in terms of my *listening and talking to others?* It means that as the Spirit fills me—as I walk by the Spirit—I can and should teach, guide and disclose the truth to others. Likewise, others can and should do the same to me. When the Ethiopian eunuch asked for someone to guide him into an understanding of the truth of Isaiah, Philip, a Spirit-filled communicator, was there to do the job.[9] In Acts 20:20, 27 Paul summarized the essence of his previous ministry to the Ephesian elders by saying, *"I did not shrink from declaring to you anything that was profitable, and teaching you publicly and from house to house...declaring to you the whole purpose of God.* As in Acts 8:31, these words in Acts 20 are the very same words used to predict the nature of the Spirit's ministry in John 14:26 and 16:13.

The obvious parallel between Ephesians 5:18-20 and Colossians 3:16-17 allows us to draw two conclusions. First, Spirit-filled believers are Word-filled believers. Second, Spirit-filled and Word-filled believers communicate with one another. They speak, sing, teach and admonish one another. Note also the inclusion of the vertical relationship—they give thanks to God. So, when I speak to others it must be with the realization that the Spirit can speak through me to them. And I must listen carefully as well, sensitive to the fact that the Spirit may be channeling truth to me through them.

The Scriptures also comment on what the Spirit-filled believer does and does not say. For example, in Galatians 5:16 we are instructed to walk by the Spirit. When we do this, our speech will be affected. With our words we will stop biting and devouring each other (v. 15), and start loving and serving one another (vv. 13-14). Note, too, that many of the deeds of the flesh (vv. 19-21) are committed by what we say. So what happens when we allow the Spirit to control us? We produce the fruit of the Spirit (vv. 22-23). All of these qualities of life have verbal significance. Patience, for example, will be evidenced by what we say—and don't say.

One other passage is pertinent. In Ephesians 4:30 we are told not to grieve the Holy Spirit. And how do we keep from doing this? The context explains: by culling the unwholesome words from our conversation (v. 29); by leaving out the words that express bitterness, anger and slander (v. 31); and by employing words that are true, kind, tender-hearted and forgiving (vv. 25, 32). Filled with the Spirit, we have the potential to stop hiding and hurling—from God and from each other. Filled with the Spirit, we have the potential to communicate openly, honestly and appropriately.

We are finite human beings listening to an infinite divine being. We need help. Help in comprehending His truth. Help in conforming to His truth. Help in communicating His truth to others. The indwelling Holy Spirit is our Helper.

Principle #2—God's Communication Involves Man as an Active Participant

God doesn't want pious, passive spectators. He wants actively involved listeners. We aren't receivers who turn ourselves on, tune ourselves in, and relax. Active, involved listening is spoken of frequently in Scripture. For example, 1 Corinthians 2:15 states that *"he who is spiritual appraises all things."*

In verses 9 through 14 "all things" or "things" are used a number of times to refer to truth that comes to man from God. In 3:1-3 the problem underscored in the fleshly believer is his inability to receive truth. "All things" refers to truth communicated to us in God's Word. The spiritual person, that is, one in whom the Holy Spirit is at work, is an "appraiser" of this truth. The word was used in biblical times of the careful, judicial investigation that preceded a court hearing. It involves searching and probing to get at the heart of the matter. That is how God expects us to listen to Him. The spiritual person is not only a qualified receiver of the truth, but also a capable investigator of it.

James also comments on the difference between superficial and substantial listening. In 1:23 he warns against being merely a hearer. That is passive listening. That person takes a quick glance at himself in the light of the Word, and promptly forgets what he saw (1:23-24). What he should do is *look intently* at the truth and obey it (1:25). The word for "looking" is different from the one used in 1:23-24. It literally means to stoop down in order to have a close look. It is used in John 20:5, 11 of the disciple's investigation of the empty tomb. The word suggests close attention to what is being examined. Passive, uninvolved listening to God is inadequate. Believers are always to be on the alert—probing for meaning and application.

Timothy is encouraged to diligently and accurately handle the Word of truth (2 Timothy 2:15). "Diligently" means zealously and actively concerned.[10] "Handling accurately" literally means "to cut straight." It conveys the idea of precision. Timothy needs to be precise in his hermeneutics and his homiletics. Why? Because the false teachers he is dealing with aren't! Diligent attention to accurate reception and transmission demands active, personal involvement. There is no place in God's scheme for lethargic listening.

Earlier, Paul told Timothy to "take pains" with the truth; to be "absorbed" in it (1 Timothy 4:15). You can't take pains with something or be absorbed in it and remain passively aloof. You must get involved. You have to open up and let God talk with the real, inner you. You have to concentrate. You have to work at stripping away all the prejudice and presuppositions that keep you from being an active, receptive listener. This is the kind of openness that the Bereans had *"for they received the word with great eagerness, examing the Scriptures daily, to see whether these things were so"* (Acts 17:11).[11]

What does this mean in terms of my *listening to God?* When I read and study the Word, I must put everything else aside and concentrate on what He is saying to me. I must give Him my undivided attention. I should do this on a regular basis, for that is the only way I can develop my listening skills. I should do this at a time when I am most alert and able to concentrate. I should do this in a place where I have minimal distractions. I should read and meditate out loud and take notes and ask questions, for these are the kinds of things that make me an active participant.

I should *observe* carefully to whom God is speaking, what He is saying and why He says it. I should *interpret* accurately what God means. I should *apply* these truths personally and practically in my own life.

It is so easy to settle for exposure to truth. We can do this by reading a verse at mealtimes, or a chapter on rising or before retiring, or by memorizing portions of Scripture. There is nothing wrong with any of these, but we can engage in them without really listening to God. On occasion, after hurried devotions, I can't even remember what I just read. Or where I read. I have settled for superficial exposure. God wants examination to go along with it. My examination of the truth. The truth's examination of me. There is no short-cut or work-free way to listen to God.

What does this mean in terms of my *listening to others?* First, I listen carefully. God may be using them to channel His truth to me. The Bible makes it clear that others in the body of Christ have the potential to teach me, encourage me, exhort me, stimulate me, edify me, reprove me, restore me.[12] If I don't pay attention to what others have to say, I may miss out on God's message to me. This takes effort on my part. I must concentrate on the words of the preacher, the Sunday School teacher, the study group leader, the voice on radio or tape, the individual on television, the printed page, the counselor, the parent, the child, the friend. There are times when God speaks through someone I don't even know, through words that are not even addressed to me. My spiritual antenna must always be up.

A second reason for listening to others is to assess their needs and thus better know what truth God wants us to communicate to them. It is not easy to give others our undivided attention. (Except when we are hurling at them!) Our minds wander. We don't remember names. We look interested but shift into neutral or some other gear that takes us off in a totally different direction from the topic at hand. While "listening" we evaluate the past, plan the future, and more often than not, decide what we will say next that will amuse or impress our friends or correct or convince our antagonist. Thoreau said it: "The greatest compliment a man ever paid me was when he asked me a question and then listened to my answer."

Listening doesn't come easily or naturally. Why? Because we are self-centered. It is natural to talk—especially about oneself. It is easy to listen—to words that flatter us. But to listen to the heartaches and burdens of others; to listen to their suggestions and criticisms; to listen in such a way that we get to know them and ourselves better—this takes work. Let's face it. We are lazy listeners.

We come in contact with such a variety of people. Pastor, parishioner, wife, husband, children, parent, brother, sister, client, patient, customer, student, teacher, salesman, mechanic, secretary, boss, employee, leader, follower, aggressive, withdrawn, confident, insecure. They are all different. We cannot preset our receiver, turn it on and assume everyone we listen to is on the same frequency. Each person has his own frequency. Some will change frequencies during a given conversation. There may be static that needs to be filtered out. We must pay constant attention to our fine-tuning dial. One never takes "time-out" to listen.

In terms of *talking to others* the implications are obvious. We who are senders must do everything to activate the receivers. Especially since human receivers have a tendency to hide. We must employ methods that stimulate people to judiciously investigate the Word. They must be motivated and trained to explore and discover truth for themselves—to hear from God first-hand. They must learn to listen for both information and insight. We must utilize the methods and media that facilitate active listening. Visual aids, dialogue, discussion, role playing, case studies, agree-disagree statements, homework, tests, etc., encourage an audience to creatively listen. Much of our communication suffers from what Reuel Howe calls "the monological illusion." We think that all we need to do is speak and others will automatically hear what we say and understand what we mean. That, my friend, is an illusion!

A word to the professional listener. That includes some of us all of the time. Listen attentively. Intensively. Interact. Ask questions. Probe meaning. Explore implications. When a communicator seeks to employ techniques aimed at making you an active participant, steadfastly resist your tendency to "just sit and listen." It may be more comfortable, but less profitable. It is nice to sit and soak up the truth like a sponge. That's fine, but sponges work better when they are squeezed. So, squeeze yourself now and then and let others squeeze you too.

Principle #3—God Communicates Everything We Need to Know

God doesn't tell us everything we *want* to know. There are secret things that belong to Him (Deuteronomy 29:29). He does reveal all we *need* to know. As new creatures in Christ, God wants us to engage in good works (Ephesians 2:10). We need to know what these good works are and how to do them. That is precisely what God communicates to us in His Word. Second Timothy 3:16-17 informs us that all Scripture is from God and, as such, is profitable for teaching, reproof, correction, and training in righteousness, and the ultimate purpose of the Scripture is to equip the man of God for every good work. It is in the Scripture we find out what these good works are and how to do them. Titus 2:11-12 presents a similar concept. God graciously saves us and then instructs us how to live here and now.

In both 2 Timothy 3:16-17 and Titus 2:11-12 what God tells us has both positive and negative connotations. He gives us teaching, training in righteousness, and insight on how to live sensibly, righteously and godly. These are all positive aspects of life that we need to know about. He also shares reproof, correction, and insight on denying ungodliness and worldly desires. These are negative factors. We need that too. God is a balanced communicator.

As a parent I seek to tell my children what they need to know in order to be the kind of persons they want to be. Sometimes what they need to know is not what they want to hear. But my main concern for their ultimate maturity must take precedence over their concern for their immediate happiness. God has that same concern for His children and therefore always tells what we need to know.

How does this affect my *listening to God?* First, it causes me to listen carefully to *everything* God says. He doesn't preface His remarks with unimportant chit chat. No small talk with God. We don't have to wait for God to get to the point. He is always at the point. In some way, everything God says is designed to meet my needs. This is what Paul has in

mind when he tells the Corinthian believers that the Old
Testament was written for their instruction (1 Corinthians
10:11).

Second, since God always speaks to my need, the better I
listen, the better I understand myself and my need. Some
needs I am keenly aware of. Others I am only vaguely conscious of. Some I don't realize exist. His truth helps me meet
the needs I am aware of and helps me face the needs I should
be aware of.

Third, I will recognize the limitations of God's communication to me. I can't expect answers to all my questions.
Nor solutions to all my problems. Nor complete insight on
crucial issues. God doesn't tell me everything I want to know.
Only what I need to know. I am grateful He chooses to tell
me as much as He does—for as the heavens are higher than
the earth so are His thoughts higher than mine (Isaiah 55:9).

Finally, I will look for both the positive and negative. I
will expect praise and criticism. I may not always *feel* good as
a result of listening to God, but eventually I will *be* good as a
result of receiving His truth.

God tells us what we need to know. How does this fit in
with my *listening to others?* He may choose to transmit the
words we need through someone else. God uses many different people to publish the truth He has authored and wants
us to receive.

For example, God uses parents to communicate truth to
children (Ephesians 6:4). The appropriate response for
children is to listen and heed because Dad and Mom are telling them what they need to know. This listening-heeding concept is imbedded in the biblical injunction given to children to
obey their parents (Ephesians 6:1). *To obey* literally means in
the Greek *to hear under*. That is what obedience is. Hearing
the instructions and voluntarily putting oneself under their
authority.

All of us are in relationships where others have biblical
justification for telling us what we need to know and do. Our
responsibility is to listen carefully. This would be true in our

relationship to civil government, to employers, to husbands, to church leaders and even to believers who, though not in a position of elected leadership, are still qualified to teach and admonish us with the truth we need to know.[13] Since God can be involved in any of these relationships, we will hear the negative as well as the positive, which is not always what we want. But it is what we need.

Now, let's develop some of the implications of this principle for *talking with others*. First, I need to get to know people. The better I know a person, the better I can speak to his needs. Friendship is basic to fellowship. The letters of Paul in the New Testament are a good case in point. It is obvious that he is writing to people that he knows and loves. He opens and closes his letters with personal, intimate, tender remarks.[14] He refers to many specific, real life situations.[15] He calls people by their names.[16] The rest of the words that he weaves into this fabric of friendship are the truths from God which they need to know. He does it well because he knows them well. That is why God can be classified as the Master Communicator. He knows us perfectly. We should work toward that goal, recognizing that the more we get next to people, the better we get through to people.

The second implication builds on the first one. As I get to know people, I should find out what they need. There is a place for chit chat and small talk. It helps to get acquainted. We use it to establish and develop relationships. But to be God's communicators we must get through that outer layer of friendship into the inner reality of fellowship. Don't forget—people tend to hide. One of the basic things they hide is their needs. You see, if we were perfect we wouldn't have any needs. Since we aren't we do. And we also have an innate propensity to hide these needs. Others are just like we are, so we have to get close to them in need-level relationships. Friendship is where we feel free to share our needs and they feel free to share theirs.

People have all kinds of needs. The need for care, concern, compassion, help, guidance, discipline, wisdom, challenge, caution, encouragement, appreciation, acceptance, etc. Through our words God wants to speak to these needs. That's why husbands and wives ought to stay close to one another. Parents to their children. Teachers to their students. Pastors to their people. Develop the kinds of relationships with people so that you know when something is bothering them and when you ask them what's bothering them, they will tell you.

Obviously Paul knew Timothy's real needs. He knew he was a bit timid, self-conscious of his youthfulness, struggling with false teachers, having a stomach problem, wondering about money. He told Timothy what he needed to know about these issues.[17]

The third implication continues the process to its logical conclusion. I get to know people. I find out what they need. *I speak to their needs.* That is, I share with them in an open, honest and appropriate way what they need to know. Once in awhile we by-pass the first two steps and start with the third one. We rush into a situation without taking time to get to know the person and become aware of their real needs. We drop the truth on them. Knowing the Word does give us insight into speaking to the needs of people. But knowing people's needs sharpens that insight and allows us to focus the Word more accurately on specific, personal needs.

Here are some examples from the Word of God that relate truth to needs:

> *"And let our people also learn to engage in good deeds to meet pressing **needs**, that they may not be unfruitful"* (Titus 3:14).

Good deeds include what we say, and what we say is oriented toward personal, pressing needs. To do less is to be unfruitful. "Have you got a minute?" No, as a matter of fact, you don't. But you sense an urgency in the question, an urgency created by a pressing need; and you pause and invest some quality time with the person. Even if you never utter a word of counsel, you are telling them something they need to know—someone loves them enough to listen to them.

"But we do not want you to be uninformed, brethren, about those who are asleep, that you may not grieve, as do the rest who have not hope" (1 Thessalonians 4:13).

Here we have needy people. They are uninformed and griev- ing. Paul decides that a dimension of their grief-need can be met by telling them what they need to know about the resur- rection of believers at the second coming of Christ. These people needed more than their tears dried. They needed their minds enlightened.

*"Now as to the love of the brethren, you have **no need** for anyone to write you, for you are taught by God to love one another"* (1 Thessalonians 4:9).

This is terrific! Believers listening to God so well that they don't need any more instruction about love right now. So notice what Paul does. He meets other needs. Their need for affirmation with a word of praise. Their need to grow with a word of challenge (v. 10). No matter whom you are with or what the situation is, you can always speak to needs. There is always something you can tell them that they need to know.

God tells us what we need to know and in so doing meets our needs. Our responsibility is to be sensitive to oppor- tunities to do the same thing. We don't always follow through. Sometimes we are so concerned about our *own needs* that we can't turn our attention to others. There's that self-centeredness coming in again. A certain degree of in- trospection is biblical and healthy. But introspection that stifles a need-oriented interest in others is wrong. It is another form of hiding. Philippians 2:4 captures the delicate balance we are to maintain. *"Do not merely look out for your own personal interests, but also for the interests of others."* The

Bible doesn't say: "When you get it all together in your own life, then reach out and relate to others." We are to work on both at the same time, and incidentally, relating to others helps us to make internal progress.

Fear also keeps us quiet. We are afraid of saying the wrong thing. So we say nothing. Or something superficial. There is that perfectionist tendency cropping up again. "I won't say anything until I can say it perfectly." Forget it! You are an imperfect communicator. You always have been. You always will be. Instead of taking a vow of *silence,* take a vow of *saturation.* Vow to saturate yourself with the Word of God. Then when you respond with words that others need to hear, they will be words from your mouth, springing from the meditations of your heart, all of which will be acceptable in God's sight (Psalm 19:14).

God doesn't expect you to be a perfect communicator. Even Paul, the articulate apostle, told the Corinthians that he didn't communicate to them with superior speech or persuasive words of wisdom. Instead he spoke to them in weakness, in fear and in much trembling (1 Corinthians 2:1-5). God expects us to be faithful, sensitive, loving sharers of His truth. On occasion, the most appropriate word you could share, the truth they need to hear from you—will be a *word of apology.* That too, can meet someone's need. It will underscore your imperfection and enhance your credibility.

Principle #4—God Communicates without Hurling

Hurling is saying the wrong thing, in the wrong way, at the wrong time. God doesn't do this. He doesn't blow His stack, fly off the handle, throw a fit, rant and rave, pout or lose control. He isn't obnoxious, overbearing or sarcastic.

This makes God sound pretty placid. Not so. He acts and reacts. The general thrust of His responses is that of being *"compassionate and gracious, slow to anger and abounding in lovingkindness,"* a lovingkindness that is everlasting.[18] "Compassionate...gracious...lovingkindness" all show that there is a basic *tenderness* in God's pattern of communication. "Slow to anger" shows that there can also be a *toughness* in what He says.

Tenderness springs from His love. Toughness springs from His justice. Because He is longsuffering we experience much of His tenderness. Because He is holy and we aren't, we experience some of His toughness. God can and will get tough with man. *"Depart from Me, accursed ones, into the eternal fire"* are the words of absolute rejection which will be directed to unbelievers by God at the time of judgment (Matthew 25:41). The believer will never hear such words of rejection from God, but we will hear words of reproof and correction.

What about anger? Does God experience it and express it? Certainly. He spoke words in anger to Israel (Numbers 32:10-15). Christ sternly rebuked Peter (Mark 8:33). In each case the right thing was being said, in the right way and at the right time. God can and will talk tough to His people. But when He does, they aren't improper, inaccurate words from a frustrated person who has lost control of himself. They are the carefully measured words of the one Person who has every right to tell it like it is.

So when we listen to God we can expect to hear a broad spectrum of conversation—from the tender to the tough. Yet no matter how perturbed He is with us, we can always be assured that He is not trying to drive us away from Him, but to draw us back to Him. Whether He is talking tough or tender, our best approach is to listen. Don't talk back. Anyway you look at it, He will have the last word.

Others will talk tough to us. Listen carefully. It could be God at work admonishing us. People will also hurl at us. They will criticize, ridicule, embarrass and misrepresent us. How should we respond?

Don't retaliate. Christ didn't. *"Being reviled, He did not revile in return; while suffering, He uttered no threats, but kept entrusting Himself to Him who judges righteously."* (1 Peter 2:23). He turned retaliation over to God the Father. We should do the same. The patience we need to endure these verbal darts will be provided by the indwelling Holy Spirit (Galatians 5:22).

In the meantime we suffer silently. Right? Wrong! First Peter three pinpoints two valid responses to verbal putdowns. First, instead of *"returning evil for evil, or insult for insult,"* give a *blessing* (3:9, cf. 1 Corinthians 4:12). Second, be *"ready to make a defense to everyone who asks you to give an account for the hope that is in you, yet with gentleness and reverence"* (3:15). Insults merit a blessing. A blessing stimulates inquiry. Inquiry merits an explanation.

How about anger? If God experiences and expresses it, does that sanction it for us? Ephesians 4:26 has succinct words on the subject. *"Be angry and yet do not sin; do not let the sun go down on your wrath."* The first clause has two imperatives. One is positive: "be angry." The Scriptures do not highlight anger as a key quality the Christian is to cultivate, so the positive imperative is viewed as an imperative of permission or concession. Anger is not something you should engage in as a way of life. It is something you could exhibit when the situation requires it. What about Ephesians 4:31? It says that all anger is to be put away. That is right. All anger that is rooted in bitterness and displayed with malice and slander is wrong. Then what anger is right? The kind God has: reaction to sin. The kind Christ had when He drove the moneychangers out of the temple (Matthew 21:12, 13). The kind David had when he talked about hating those who hated God (Psalm 139:21). For an extended discourse from an angry Lord note Christ's denunciation of the scribes and Pharisees in Matthew 23. Anger can be a legitimate behavioral response for the biblically sensitive Christian. The news of a kidnapping, a rape, a child beating makes us angry. Rightly so.

The second imperative is a prohibition: "and yet do not sin." Anger can easily overflow its biblical banks, become sin and do a lot of damage. Our tendency is to hide angry reactions and allow them to smolder internally. Gradually they eat away at the biblical boundaries and seep into the sinful attitudes and actions spoken of in verse 31. Therefore, don't let the sun go down on your anger. Handle it properly and quickly. The day of anger should be the day of reconciliation. Furthermore, to nurse a grudge is to make oneself vulnerable to the deceptions of Satan (v. 27).

The primary implication we should draw from the fact that God does not hurl is that since we are to be like Him, we should not hurl. The Holy Spirit can produce in us conversational patience, kindness and gentleness (Galatians 5:22, 23). He can tame our tongues and produce words of wisdom from above that are peaceable, gentle, reasonable and full of mercy (James 3:1-18). One of the marks of maturity is the ability to discern good and evil (Hebrews 5:14). This comes as a result of training ourselves to apply the Word in situations that require such discernment (Hebrews 5:13, 14). When tempted to say the wrong thing in the wrong way at the wrong time to the hurt and alienation of other people, the Holy Spirit desires to help us discern the character (good or evil) of our thoughts and proposed words. He can also enable us to change so that the words of our mouth and the meditations of our heart are acceptable in God's sight (Psalm 19:14).

Recently, my family and I went on a vacation trip. As we communicated our personal preferences as to when to eat, where to eat, what to eat and when to stop and look for a motel room, and which motel to choose, and who was going to sleep where, and who sits in the back seat and who sits in the front—there was some hurling—from all of us. We had to work hard at discerning the character of our responses to one another. Sometimes we spoke first and discerned later! That is the way life is for us. Every day presents a variety of opportunities to hurl. As we allow the Spirit to apply the Word, we will know how and when to speak the truth in love and thus communicate to instruct, encourage and inspire, rather than to injure and incite. We can be concerned, confident, incisive communicators without being hostile, obnoxious and offensive.

Principle #5—God Communicates to Critique

He wants to inform us *and* to critique us. We enjoy information. We avoid critique. God intends for both to happen. The same truth that teaches and trains us—reproves and corrects us (2 Timothy 3:16). Hebrews 4:12, 13 presents this concept in a graphic way:

> *"For the word of God is living and active and sharper than any two-edged sword, and piercing as far as the division of soul and spirit, of both joints and marrow, and able to judge the thoughts and intentions of the heart. And there is no creature hidden from His sight, but all things are open and laid bare to the eyes of Him with whom we have to do."*

The preceding context is an exhortation to believers to enter into the faith-rest life. To fail to do so, as Israel did, is to be disobedient (4:6, 11). We can know these truths, and know whether we are obeying them because God communicates them in a unique, personal way. Verses 12 and 13 tell us how.

"The word of God is living and active." Revelation partakes of the character of the Revealer. He is alive. His Word is alive. It is also active. The Greek word is *energes,* from which we get our word *energy.* God's message is not alive and static. It is alive and dynamic. Our old dog is alive and static. She mostly lies around and sleeps. A puppy is alive and dynamic. The Word is active, not passive. It goes forth to accomplish a task.[19] Sermons and Sunday School lessons are sometimes dull and dead. That is not God's fault. Preachers and teachers are the lines through which this high voltage truth is transmitted. Sometimes we act as step-down transformers. What a travesty!

"Sharper than any two-edged sword." The Word is designed to pierce. Pierce what? The shell. The facade. The mask. The exterior walls we put up and hide behind. God's Word has a definite point to it. He doesn't confront by moving *up close* to us. He confronts by moving *into* us.

"Piercing as far as the division of soul and spirit, of both joints and marrow." The Word is fashioned to pierce, penetrate and probe. Soul and spirit are two of the prime biblical aspects of our immaterial, psychological nature. Joints and marrow are aspects of our material, physiological makeup. This, however, is not primarily a treatise on human psychology and physiology. It is an indication of the extent to which the Word probes the inner man. The material and the immaterial constitute me—the total person. That is where the Word does its job.

"Able to judge the thoughts and intentions of the heart." The Word probes with purpose. "Able to judge" is the Greek word *kritikos,* which means "to sift out and analyze evidence." Our English words *criticize, critical* and *critique* are rooted in this term. Now you can see even more clearly why we say the Word is not simply to instruct, but also to critique. "Thoughts" and "intentions" are essentially synonymous terms in the Greek language. They refer to the human activity of pondering, reflecting and thinking. The emphasis is on the mind, but the emotions and the will are closely involved. The "heart" is that all-embracing term that refers to the human personality in general or to certain aspects of it in particular. Here it is another way of referring to the total inner man.

"No creature hidden from His sight." We can hide from family, friends and neighbors, but not from God. With x-ray like power His Word can probe into the inner recesses of anyone's life.

"All things are open and laid bare to the eyes of Him with whom we have to do." No one can hide from Him. Everything that is true about us is "open," literally in the Greek, "naked." Before Him all the superficial cover-up is stripped away. Before Him and His Word we appear just as we really are. All of our attitudes, negative and positive, are focused in the light of His truth. "Laid bare" is the Greek word *trachelizo.* From the noun *trachelos* we get our term *trachea,* which is the wind pipe, the tube through which air

passes to and from the lungs. In New Testament days *trachelos* referred to the neck or throat and the verb *trachelizo* meant "to grab by the throat." It was used, for example, of a wrestler's stranglehold on his opponent's throat. The concept here is that we are not only open but vulnerable when confronted by God. To listen carefully to God in His Word is to allow Him to strip us and take us by the throat and talk to us. When He does that, there will be real confrontation, for we will be, in a sense, looking Him in the eye. And so the verse closes with the fact that we are open and laid bare *to the eyes* of Him with whom we have to do—or, more literally, to whom we must give an account.

When a parent really wants to confront his child with the fact of his suspected wrongdoing, how does he go about it? "Look me right square in the eye!" he says. The eyes are the windows of the soul. Such an encounter is very intimate, and can be, for the guilty one, very intimidating. This is how God wants to communicate with us—a person-to-person, face-to-face, eye-to-eye encounter.

What are the implications for us as listeners? God wants to speak to the real, inner me. He is not satisfied with a shallow, impersonal conversation. He communicates to evaluate. We have not really listened to God until our lives have been critiqued. A lot of Bible reading, Bible study, Scripture memory, preaching, teaching and counseling falls short of this. Unless the Word is critically examining my life, its purpose is being thwarted.

God's evaluation will call attention to what is right and wrong. It is pleasant to be commended. It is painful to be corrected. There will be times when the truth hurts. An interesting sidelight of this is that the more I listen to God at this level, the more I will learn how to accept *praise* and *criticism*. I will begin to understand that I cannot grow without both of them. I will begin to understand how to respond to both of them—give thanks. That is what I am to do in everything (1 Thessalonians 5:18). This has provided me much insight in knowing how to respond to the praise and criticism of others.

When their words are legitimate, a simple but significant "thank you" is all that is needed, whether I am responding to praise or criticism. When God tells me in His Word that I am an important and significant person, my tendency is to play it down, just like I feel uncomfortable when a student tells me a class presentation was superb. The appropriate response is simply "thank you." When God's Word indicts my failure, again I feel uncomfortable and want to squirm away from the pressure of criticism, just as I do when my wife calls attention to the fact that the chore I promised to do three days ago is still undone. The appropriate response is "thank you," followed by whatever action needs to be taken.

God will channel truth through others to critique us. Paul realized that he was carrying out such a function in the lives of the Corinthians. He had written them a letter of strong criticism. It caused them to sorrow; it hurt them (2 Corinthians 7:8). The final outcome was that they were made sorrowful to the point of repentance, and Paul rejoiced in that (v. 9). He was putting into effect the philosophy of ministry he states in Colossians 1:28: *"Admonishing every man and teaching every man with all wisdom, that we may present every man complete in Christ."* "Admonishing" means "to show what it is wrong." When you show someone what is wrong, you critique him; and it may hurt, but you are not doing it to get even. You are doing it to help him grow. Paul goes on to say that all those in the Colossian church were to be *"teaching and admonishing one another"* (Colossians 3:16). It is our responsibility to develop the kind of relationship with the Lord that gives us the *maturity* to admonish others, and the kinds of relationships with others that give us the *right* to admonish them. Then we can speak the truth in love.

What happens when God uses someone else to critique us? Like a wife, or a husband, or a friend? If our ego armor bristles defensively, it may be an indication that we have not been allowing God to call attention to our faults and failures. When God is consistently evaluating my life I am not nearly as threatened by others who do the same to me. If I am supersensitive to criticism and terribly threatened by evaluation, it could be a good indication that I am not listening to everything God wants to tell me about myself.

In Summary

We have explored five communication principles. Each one related to how God communicates to us. The implications for our own communication patterns with God and others were developed. The five principles were:

1. God's Communication Involves the Holy Spirit—the resident Teacher who helps us understand and transmit the truth.
2. God's Communication Involves Man as an Active Participant—listening to God is more than a passive act; it is an active art.
3. God Communicates Everything We Need to Know— that means it is all important, personalized truth.
4. God Communicates without Hurling—He is never working out His problems; He is working on our problems.
5. God Communicates to Critique—we may have to feel bad in order to become good.

Interaction

1. "I listen to God first; then I listen to others." Do you agree? Should these two steps be sequential—the former always preceding the latter? Or are they mutually reinforcing and thus should occur simultaneously?

2. "I don't get much out of the sermon." What are some of the reasons a person would make this statement?

3. Why doesn't God tell us everything we want to know? What are some of the things you would like to know that you don't think God has revealed in His Word?

4. Which is more important—to know the Scriptures or to know people?

5. A good communicator will not hide, hurl or hurt. Discuss.

6. In teaching these principles, make sure the student not only understands each principle and its biblical basis, but also sees the practical implications of it for life. Case studies could be developed to help learners interact with the principles. One could be set up, for example, which depicted someone putting one or more of these principles into effect. Students would then examine the case study looking for the positive factors present in the situation. Another case study might present one or more of these principles being misused or unused. The teacher might also direct the students to certain Scriptures dealt with in this chapter and have them

extract vertical and horizontal communication principles from the biblical passages.

Footnotes

[1]Genesis 1:26; Psalm 103:20; Job 1:7; Genesis 3:9; 1 Corinthians 2:9-10; Psalm 19:1-6; Romans 1:18-20; Hebrews 1:1-3; John 1:1, 14-18; 2 Timothy 3:16-17.
[2]Romans 5:5; 8:9; 16; 1 Corinthians 6:19.
[3]John 14:17; 15:26.
[4]John 14:16, 26.
[5]John 14:26; 15:26; 16:13.
[6]John 16:14.
[7]Ephesians 5:18; Galatians 5:16.
[8]1 Corinthians 2:9-16; Ephesians 6:17.
[9]Acts 8:26-40.
[10]Note what else the believer is to be diligently doing: Ephesians 4:3; Hebrews 4:11; 2 Peter 1:10; 3:14.
[11]"Examine" is the same Greek word translated "appraise" in 1 Corinthians 2:15.
[12]Matthew 18:15-17; Romans 15:14; Galatians 6:1; Ephesians 4:15-16; Colossians 3:16; 1 Thessalonians 5:11; Hebrews 10:24-25.
[13]Romans 13:1-8; Ephesians 6:5-8; Colossians 3:18; Hebrews 13:17; Ephesians 4:15-16; Colossians 3:16; Galatians 6:1.
[14]Philippians 1:3-11; 1 Corinthians 16:10-24.
[15]1 Corinthians 1:10-17; Philippians 4:2.
[16]Romans 16:1-27.
[17]2 Timothy 1:7; 1 Timothy 4:12; 1:3; 5:23; 6:10.
[18]Psalms 103:8; 100:5; 136:1-26.
[19]Isaiah 55:11; Jeremiah 23:29; 1 Peter 1:23.

Resources

1. For insight on personal Bible study: *The Joy of Discovery in Bible Study* by Oletta Wald, Augsburg Publishing House, 1975.
2. For insight on listening: *A Listener's Guide to Preaching* by William D. Thompson, Abingdon Press, 1966.
3. For insight on talking: *Caring Enough To Confront* by David W. Augsburger, Regal Books, 1973.
4. For insight on the Holy Spirit: *The Holy Spirit in your Teaching* by Roy B. Zuck, Scripture Press, 1963.

Chapter 7

Talking to God

A good communicator talks well and listens well. God does both. In the previous chapter we focused on God's Word to us and our responsibility to listen well. Now we turn our attention to God's listening to us and our responsibility to talk well.

Talking to God. We call it—*prayer.*

Prayer is that privilege and responsibility we have of talking with our heavenly Father. It is not our purpose here to develop all that the Bible teaches about prayer. What we want to do is look at prayer as communication and discover how we can communicate more effectively with God in prayer and see what impact this will have on our conversation with others. As in the previous chapter, we will set up principles and relate them to how we talk to God and how we talk and listen to others.

I am amazed at how much information the airline ticket clerk can get from his computer. That is because he knows his computer. He knows what the computer can do for him. And most significantly, he knows how to talk to the computer. He does it by pushing the right keys.

God is loaded with data the believer needs. And we need

to know Him. We need to know what He can do for us. We need to know how to talk to Him. But God is more than a data-bank. He is a person. We can know Him through Christ. We can make this relationship more meaningful by talking to Him. The more the ticket clerk knows about how his computer listens, the better he can talk to it. The more we know about how God listens, the better we can talk to Him.

The following diagram visualizes the premise we are working on. The more I understand how God listens to me, the better equipped I am to know how I should talk to Him.

I Speak to God

Don't forget that our relationship with God can never be separated from our relationships with other human beings. As I develop my skills in talking with God this should affect my ability to talk to man.

Furthermore, as I become more aware of how God listens to me, I will be developing some practical guidelines on how I should listen to others.

In other words, growth in my prayer life should make me a better talker and a better listener. The Bible says we are to be "imitators of God" (Ephesians 5:1). What we are doing is exploring God as a communicator so we can better know how to imitate His talking and listening patterns.

Principle #1—Communication with God Involves the Holy Spirit

The Spirit who enables us to understand the word *from* God also helps us utter our words *to* God. We are exhorted to *"pray at all times in the Spirit"* (Ephesians 6:18; Jude 20). No further explanation is given in these two references as to what it means to pray in the Spirit. We know that He indwells us (Romans 8:16). We know that He empowers us (Acts 1:8). We know that He teaches us (John 14:26). So to pray in the Spirit would certainly include believing in His personal presence while we pray, depending on His power in our prayers, and applying His truth to our prayers.

Romans 8:26, 27 is the only other passage that speaks clearly to praying in the Holy Spirit.

> *"And in the same way the Spirit also helps our weakness; for we do not know how to pray as we should, but the Spirit Himself intercedes for us with groanings too deep for words; and He who searches the hearts knows what the mind of the Spirit is, because He intercedes for the saints according to the will of God."*

The preceding context (vv. 18-25) deals with the suffering the whole creation and all Christians are currently experiencing. Though we "groan" under this burden, we have the *"first fruits of the Spirit"* (v. 23) which gives us a confident hope for our eventual glorification. In the same way that the indwelling Spirit gives *hope* for the present suffering, verse 26 reveals that He also gives us *help* in present suffering.

Help for what? Our weakness. What weakness? We have many, but the one that this verse calls attention to is the fact that *"we do not know how to pray."* The right kind of prayer doesn't come naturally or easily. On our own we need help in knowing what to pray and how to pray. We don't understand the problems we encounter. We don't know what solutions to ask for. We can all put together pious cliches and vain repetitions. That is not our problem. Our problem is knowing what to ask for as we suffer in a sinful world. Knowing what will meet our needs and at the same time be in God's will.

"As we should" points out that there is a right way to pray. Prayer is not random firing at blurred moving targets. There are some specific things we need to know and do with regard to prayer.

The Spirit is present to "help" us in this regard. This is the double compound Greek word *sunantilambano*. The Greek scholar, A.T. Robertson, says this about the word: "The Holy Spirit lays hold of our weakness along with (*sun*) us and carries His part of the burden facing us (*anti*) as if two men were carrying a log, one at each end."[1] The only other place in the New Testament this word occurs is in Luke 10:40 where Martha expresses her need for help in the kitchen.

Our weakness has been defined as *ignorance*. His help is defined as *"interceding for us with groanings too deep for words."* "Intercede" is in the present tense, showing this to be a continuing work in the believer. He comes to our aid by means of "groanings"—a reference to internal feelings—the kind of response we express with a deep sigh or a meaningful shrug of the shoulders. Creation groans (v. 22). The Christian groans (v. 23), but the Christian does not groan alone! These groanings are not expressed in words, nevertheless God searches our hearts and hears them and knows what their intent is. He is aware that the Spirit will articulate only that which is according to the will of God for the saint.

This passage teaches us that we need help in our prayer life, and that the Holy Spirit provides it. Some of our problems are so complex they are beyond words. The Spirit will help us communicate even wordless prayers to God, and God will know exactly what is being said. The Spirit will always pray according to the will of God for the believer. Verse 28 adds that though we may not know how to pray, we do know whom we are praying to—and He causes all things to work together for good—even those things we consider bad.

Is this a private conversation between two members of the Trinity using a channel we cannot get on and a code we cannot break? Or is it a tiny morsel of profound insight about how the Spirit works in, with and through us in communicating with God? A morsel we can add to our understanding of the Holy Spirit and prayer, or something we should set aside as totally irrelevant for our experience? We need to take time to explore these questions.

We are certainly involved very personally in the experience of suffering and groaning (vv. 18, 23). Likewise we experience the Spirit's provision of hope and we personally "wait eagerly" for our future redemption (vv. 23-25). If the Spirit helps us in our prayer life "in the same way" (v. 26), then we must in some way be personally, actively involved in it. This is one of the ministries that occurs in us when we are rightly related to the Spirit. The thrust of the first part of chapter eight of Romans is that the believer can and should walk according to the Spirit, set his mind on the things of the Spirit, live according to the Spirit, be led by the Spirit and listen to the inner witness of the Spirit. When we do this we will experience the Spirit's help in our prayer life. Verse 26 says that we don't know how to pray as we ought to and that the Holy Spirit steps in and helps us. This could be construed to mean that since we don't know how to pray, the Spirit will pray for us and we don't have to pray at all. Obviously, such an interpretation is incompatible with many other passages of Scripture that tell us it is our responsibility to pray. If we say that this passage means that the Spirit takes over our prayer life when we are suffering, then Paul was wrong to have kept talking to God about his thorn in the flesh (2 Corinthians 12:7-9).

Prayer is the primary focus of Romans 8:26, 27. But don't forget that the Spirit and the Word work together. As the believer goes through suffering, the Spirit will be teaching him how the Word should be applied to the situation, as well as helping him in prayer. As a matter of fact, the very act of helping us in prayer must also involve teaching, for He helps our ignorance as well as our inability. If we say that there are some situations that are so bad that even the Word cannot help us, and at that point the Spirit stops teaching and applying the Word, and does nothing but pray, then we do harm to 2 Timothy 3:16-17 where the Word is classified as that which has the capacity to make us adequate for *every* good work.

When it says that the Spirit "intercedes for us" does this mean we do not pray? Is there some point when we stop praying and turn it all over to the Spirit? Obviously not. We are to pray without ceasing (1 Thessalonians 5:17). In the midst of trials when we are confused and lack wisdom we are still exhorted to pray (James 1:2-8).

Just as with Philippians 2:13 (*"God at work in you"*) we must take into account Philippians 2:12 (*"Work out your own salvation"*), so along with Romans 8:26-27 we must take into account the many other Scriptures that relate to the Holy Spirit, the believer and prayer.

We have already seen that we *groan* (v. 23). The conclusion we are coming to is that we can groan with the Spirit, or to put it another way, the Spirit can be significantly involved in our groaning—helping us to formulate its content and helping us to direct it toward God the Father. Yet this is prayer *"too deep for words."* The groanings are not expressed in articulated speech. It does not mean that the groanings are irrational and devoid of thoughtful content. There are simply times when the situation is so intense, the problem is so involved, and solutions seem so ineffectual that words fail us. But the problem is still there and we must deal with it. At this critical moment of our experience, the Holy Spirit helps us. He helps us take our melancholy meditation and apply the truth to it in such a way that it becomes a more fruitful pondering—*biblical brooding*—we might call it. Brooding, as any hen knows, can be a most productive experience. Then we pray. Where we cannot—because of our finiteness and imperfection—put it into words, the Holy Spirit intercedes for us. Like a senior editor would add clarifying remarks to the work of a cub reporter, so the Spirit may augment our concerns and crystallize them for the One who searches our hearts.

Principle #2—Communication with God involves Man as an Active Participant

Through his Bible study, man is to be an active receiver. In prayer, man is to be an active sender. The Scriptures exhort us to ask, seek and knock (Matthew 7:7). To do this we must be actively involved. The Word establishes this fact in a variety of ways. We will briefly mention some of them.

The Lord warned His disciples about using meaningless repetition in one's prayer life (Matthew 6:7). He was against thoughtless prayer, where our mouths are in gear but our minds are in neutral. We are to pray with persistence and not give up easily (Luke 11:5-10; 18:1-8). The tax-gatherer was commended for his self-humbling that took place in his brief, personal, pointed prayer (Luke 18:11-14). The Pharisee who remained detached and self-deceived during his prayer was soundly condemned (Luke 18:9-10). Prayer is not to be mechanical and impersonal.

Paul's prayers were models of personal involvement. They sprang from his "heart's desire" (Romans 10:1). They related to the specific, personal needs of others (Philippians

1:9-11; Colossians 1:9-12). He urged others to do what he did—to get actively involved in prayer. The Christians at Rome were asked *"to strive together with me in your prayers"* (Romans 15:30). The root of the word "strive" is the Greek word *agonizomai*—to carry on a conflict, a struggle. Prayer demands that we leave the sidelines and get out on the field. Epaphras is commended for *"laboring earnestly in his prayers"* (Colossians 4:12). The Colossian believers were exhorted to avidly "devote" themselves to prayer and to stay "alert" while praying (Colossians 4:2; cf. Ephesians 6:18). The prayer instructions of Philippians 4:6 require attention to details. No room here for the vague, nebulous conversation with God.

James adds to our prayer portfolio by telling us to pray in faith (James 1:6). Active believing ties us in to what we are saying and why and to whom. In chapter four he points out that our motives are important in prayer (4:3). It is not just what we are saying but why. Finally, in chapter five: *"Is anyone among you suffering? Let him pray"* (5:13). About what? About the specific details of his personal need in suffering. "Help!" is a good start but needs more to effect a real affiliation. John instructs believers to confess their sins to God (1 John 1:9). This too, requires more than a superficial, uninvolved "I did it."

The above evidence is compiled to help us realize that (1) we ought to pray and (2) we ought to be actively and personally involved in prayer. Some don't pray at all. We need to. We cannot develop a meaningful relationship with a person if we never talk to them. Talk to God.

Some pray fairly regularly, but oh, so routinely. We fall into the routine of certain phrases. "Lord, bless us."(In what particular way?) "Lord, forgive us." (For what?) "Lord, give us wisdom." (About what?) Such phrases easily move from the conventional to the commonplace to the trite to the hackneyed. Some of us are almost addicted to certain cliches and use them with a minimum of personal involvement.

I knelt with my daughter, Juli, beside her bed one evening to have prayer with her before she went to sleep. I immediately proceeded to thank God for the food we were about to eat! Juli nudged me with her foot and informed me that it wasn't suppertime, it was bedtime. Caught red-handed in thoughtless repetition.

There is no quick, simple, easy way to pray. It takes hard work and concentration. The solution is not longer prayers. The longer the prayer the shorter the distance it travels, i.e. to those in the room. Long prayers are usually designed to teach doctrine and make announcements. It is quality conversation God wants from us.

Good conversation *with other human beings* demands the same concerted effort from us. Our tendency is to be satisfied with casual, superficial, cliche-ridden comments that pass the time rather than build relationships.

Today I met a man
But not really.
Rather, our paths crossed.
The private paths of our own
    separate worlds made a juncture
    and we were there.
We told our impersonal names
    and shook each other's hand
    warmly and firmly—to convey
    our interest
    which wasn't there.
We shared our views
    on the weather, politics,
    the latest news
    and other foreign things
    which were not there.
And when the conversation lagged,
    we said:
    "Well, glad to have met you"
    "Same here"

We lied, smiled, extended our hands
    again, and parted—
    glad to be on our separate ways
    from our little meeting.
Today I met a man
But not really.

               —Author unknown

Somebody has described our conversation as "an army of pompous phrases, moving over the landscape in search of an idea." That is often true of our conversation with others and with God.

On the other hand, those of us involved in the formal communicating professions—teachers, preachers, broadcasters, writers, etc.—will spend great amounts of time and effort in planning what we are going to say to our audience and how we are going to say it. Then when it comes to talking to God, we ad lib it and offer Him our sterile, stereotyped, bland, banal words.

Principle #3—I Can Always Have God's Undivided Attention

You will get no busy signal, no detached, glassy-eyed stare, no "let me put you on hold" from God. He is always available. He never takes a vacation. He never shuts down for remodeling. He never overbooks. His circuits are never overloaded. He is always there. David comments on God's readiness to hear in Psalm 34:

"I sought the Lord, and He answered me" (v. 4).
"This poor man cried and the Lord heard Him" (v. 6).
"The eyes of the Lord are toward the righteous, and His ears are open to their cry" (v. 15).
"The righteous cry and the Lord hears" (v. 17).

We must also hasten to add that the Scriptures make it clear that God does not hear the unrighteous.[2] The person who willfully is rejecting God and rebelling against His law has no open door invitation to speak to Him, unless the words to be spoken are words of contrition and confession.[3]

I can always have God's undivided attention. Anytime. Anywhere. Under any circumstances. That is one reason why we are exhorted to pray without ceasing (1 Thessalonians 5:17). When there is no one else to talk to—God is there. When others are busy—God is available.

The first implication is a word of *caution*. Absolute availability is something we can't really model in our own lives. God is perfect and doesn't have to take time out to refresh Himself. But we do. We cannot be all things to all people all of the time. We have to get away. To rest. To reflect. To recuperate. To concentrate on other things.

God is omnipresent. He can be everywhere at once, listening to anyone who wants to talk to Him, giving them His complete concentration. He is also omniscient and knows all the answers. We are neither omnipresent nor omniscient. It is our temptation to play God. We can't listen to everyone. We can't meet everyone's needs. We don't have the answer to everyone's questions. We must recognize our limitations and not become so involved in giving our attention to everyone else that we neglect ourselves and others who are significantly close to us and need to be listened to, e.g. members of our family.

The second implication is a word of *challenge*. In the context of our limitations we should seriously recognize our responsibility to give others our undivided attention. What God does for us; we do for others. We do have to be selective, but then we need to treat seriously those whom we select to listen to. We can't speak an edifying word that meets the needs of the moment unless we have listened carefully to find out what the need is (Ephesians 4:29). The strong cannot bear the weaknesses of those without strength unless they listen attentively to find out who the weak are and what their weaknesses are (Romans 15:1). We can best rejoice with those who rejoice and weep with those who weep as a result of hearing from them about the good and bad things in their lives

(Romans 12:15). We can miss out on the admonition and discipline we may need if we refuse to listen to the words a brother uses to confront us (Matthew 18:15). We cannot bear one another's burdens if we do not encourage them to talk to us and then listen with unrivaled attention (Galatians 6:1). What produces growth in the body? Ephesians 4:15 says it well: *"Speaking the truth in love."* Don't let the continuing emphasis on *speaking* cause us to miss the fact that if anything profitable is going to take place, all the members of the body must also be actively engaged in listening! At times our emphasis on the speaking ministries would caricaturize the body as having 300 mouths and no ears! Note how the Word of God also emphasizes the importance of *hearing*:

> *"But you did not learn Christ in this way, if indeed you **heard** Him and have been taught in Him"* (Ephesians 4:21).

> *"The things you have learned and received and **heard** and seen in me, practice these things"* (Philippians 4:9).

> *"Retain the standard of sound words which you have **heard** from me"* (2 Timothy 1:13).

> *"And the things which you have **heard** from me in the presence of many witnesses, these entrust to faithful men, who will be able to teach others also"* (2 Timothy 2:2).

> *"But let every man be quick to **hear**, slow to speak"* (James 1:19).

> *"He who has an ear, let him **hear** what the Spirit says to the churches* (Revelation 2:11).

The body grows individually and corporately, as its gifted members *speak and listen to the truth.*

Principle #4—I Can't Hide Anything from God
So why try? The 139th Psalm is a classic passage dealing with the practical implications of the omniscience and omnipresence of God. Because David knows that God is intimately acquainted with all of his ways (v. 3), he issues the invitation to *"search me, O God, and know my heart; try me and know my anxious thoughts; and see if there be any hurtful way in me, and lead me in the everlasting way"* (vv. 23, 24). We have seen in Hebrews 4:13 that *"there is no creature hidden from His sight, but all things are open and laid bare to the eyes of Him with whom we have to do."* In Romans 8:27 God is the one who *"searches the hearts."* Here are some more passages that reinforce the fact that God has intimate knowledge of us:

> *"...for the Lord searches all hearts, and understands every intent of the thoughts"* (1 Chronicles 28:9).

> *"If we had forgotten the name of our God, or extended our hands to a strange god; would not God find this out? For He knows the secrets of the heart"* (Psalm 44:20, 21).

> *"I the Lord search the heart, I test the mind, even to give to each man according to His ways, according to the result of his deeds"* (Jeremiah 17:10).

> *"...and all the churches will know that I am He who searches the minds and hearts"* (Revelation 2:23).

We cannot keep anything hidden from God. He knows what we are hiding. He knows what we have been hurling. He knows what we are thinking. What we are feeling. To play it coy with God is like a child holding something behind his back where you can't see it. God is omniscient; He sees right through us. God is omnipresent; He is looking behind us. To "keep it to yourself" when doing business with God is an illusion.

Talking with God openly can have healthy results. First, it makes us feel better. Keeping something in that needs to be shared has the same effect on us that turning up the fire has on the sealed pressure cooker. The steam has no place to go. It will ruin what is inside. Eventually it will explode—ruining what is outside. The same thing happens to us. John wrote: *"Our fellowship is with the Father, and with His Son Jesus Christ. And these things we write, so that our joy may be made complete"* (1 John 1:3, 4). Talking openly with God develops that fellowship and reaps the beneficial results—*joy*. David was talking about the same thing when he said, *"in Thy presence is fullness of joy"* (Psalm 16:11).

The second result is that once you have shared your bottled up burden with God, that may solve it and settle it. You may not need to share it with anyone else. It could be inappropriate or unnecessary to do so. You have dealt with it in a healthy way and are no longer hiding it and trying to work it through on your own.

The third result is that having opened up to God you are now better prepared, if necessary, to share it with others. If I have talked it over with God, I now have more insight on *what* to say to others and *how* to say it. If it is difficult for me to communicate things of a more personal nature with significant others, then just the process of verbalizing these things to God equips me to better verbalize them to others.

I can't hide from God. To do so is to hurt myself and to grieve God. To share openly and honestly with Him is to help myself as well as my relationship with God and others. Once in a while a troubled person will come to me and start the conversation with these words: "I've never told this to anyone before." Anyone? Not even God? That is too bad. Too bad we haven't helped believers recognize that they can and should feel free to communicate everything with God. This doesn't replace interpersonal communication at the horizontal level, but it does provide another dimension of interpersonal communication with the One who has searched us and known us (Psalm 139:1).

Principle #5—I Can Tell God Everything

You can't shock God. You can't embarrass Him. Earlier we said that we need a relationship with a person at whom we can hurl, but who gives us no cause to, and won't be alienated if we do. God is that person. We can tell Him anything and everything. Without fear of rejection. You can even hurl at God. He won't get up from His throne and say "All right Charlie—that's it. I've had all I can take from you" and stomp off to the far corner of heaven and pout, while removing Charlie from His list of preferred saints.

There is a sense in which we can *doctrinalize* Christianity so much that we *depersonalize* it. We are talking to the infinite, sovereign, majestic, righteous Creator and Lord of the universe. Right? Right! We are also talking to our Father. We are His children. There is a loving, family relationship. He is concerned about us and wants us to share anything and everything with Him.

Are you frustrated over the circumstances in your life? Feel like you need to unload? To ventilate? Nurturing some angry thoughts about the status quo? About others? About God? *Tell Him*. David did. Listen to his words in Psalm 13:

"How long, O Lord? Wilt Thou forget me forever? How long wilt Thou hide Thy face from me?" (v. 1)

(Look Lord, I've been under this pressure for a long time. I am miserable. You know what I am beginning to think? You have forgotten all about me. You say You care, but You are acting like You couldn't care less. How much more of this do You think I can take? I am just about ready to throw in the towel.)

> *"How long shall I take counsel in my soul, having sorrow in my heart all the day?"* (v. 2a)

(Every night I work out possible solutions in my mind. I try them during the day. Nothing seems to work. The problem is overwhelming me.)

> *"How long will my enemy be exalted over me?"* (v. 2b)

(Right now the problem is on top. That leaves me on the bottom. I can't take this kind of life much longer. It's not fair. I am about ready to crack under the strain.)

These honest, questioning words come from one who elsewhere in Scripture is classified as a man after God's heart (Acts 13:22). He is frustrated, depressed and miserable. He tells God exactly what he is thinking and precisely how he feels. We must hasten to add, however, that his conversation with God is not limited to the expression of negative data. In verses 3 and 4 he asks for the ability to understand the situation so he can perform well and not be a poor testimony. In verses 5 and 6 he affirms his commitment to trust in God for His past and present salvation. David didn't hide his inner feelings from God. He told God everything. So can you.

We listen with interest to the prayer of the Lord Jesus in Luke 22:42. *"Father, if Thou art willing, remove this cup from Me; yet not My will, but Thine be done."* These are very, very honest words. *"Remove this cup from me."* Why did He say this? He knew that He was facing not only the agony of crucifixion but also the trauma of taking on His sinless self the sins of the world and being separated from God the Father. This prospect created overwhelming feelings of anxiety and fear. He was, in His humanity, *scared*. These feelings gave rise to an open, honest, appropriate expression of the request not to go through with it. And remember, He was without sin. This honest desire to recoil from the cross was not wrong, but very real and appropriate. Just as appropriate as your feelings of fear before major surgery. Note, however, that in this same passage He reconfirmed His commitment to the Father's purpose and plan with the words *"yet not my will, but Thine be done."* The Lord was open and honest in His prayer life, and the commentary He made on His life was *"I always do those things that are pleasing to Him"* (the Father, John 8:29). The Spirit of God wants to reproduce that kind of life in us. Be candidly honest with God in prayer. Christ was.

We cannot tell others everything. Some things they don't need to know. Some things they can't take. Some things they won't take. Our words may depress them, confuse them, frustrate them, upset them, alienate them. No matter how close the relationship is with another person, eventually we can hurt and even destroy that relationship with our words. Only God can handle anything and everything we have to say, want to say, need to say. Deepen that relationship with God. Tell Him everything. He will never interrupt, except to inject a word of truth.

Principle #6—Communication with God Always Involves the Positive

God has a way of keeping us in balance. The opportunity to tell him everything tends to move us toward unloading on Him all of the negative things in our lives. He wants that, but He also wants to hear from us on the positive side too.

The phrase "with thanksgiving" is one of the primary ways the Bible refers to positive communication. Time and time again we are exhorted to pray "with thanksgiving."[4] Along with thanksgiving, adoration and praise are also to be included in our conversations with God.[5] Thanksgiving, adoration and praise are, by their very nature, positive. They cause us to focus on God—who He is, what He has done, what He is doing, and what He can do. This helps us to resist our inevitable tendency to focus on ourselves.

We should relate to others positively, too. Words of affection, appreciation and affirmation are always appropriate and need to be consistently expressed to others. Paul exhorted the Colossian Christians to put on a heart of compassion, kindness and gentleness (Colossians 3:12). This would cause them to say positive things to others and about others. Note how often Paul included words of thanksgiving about people in his prayers. Note further that he told them that he thanked God for them. He is giving them some subtle but very real, positive strokes![6] Paul didn't let the positive replace the negative. He told them what they needed to know, whether they wanted to hear it or not.[7] But he always included the positive word. He affirmed the Roman believers with the comment that he was *"convinced that you yourselves are full of goodness, filled with all knowledge, and able also to admonish one another"* (Romans 15:14). He thanked the Philippians for their gift to him (Philippians 4:10ff). He told the Thessalonians that he proudly recommended their example of faith and love to other churches he visited (2 Thessalonians 1:4).

Check out your own communication patterns. How much of your conversation with God includes genuine praise and thanksgiving, adoration and gratitude? Are you light on these factors and heavy on the problems and needs you and others have? When you talk with others, how would you rate yourself in terms of the positive? How often each day do you express words of affection to your marriage partner? What about the children? You call attention to their poor behavior. Rightly so. Do you give equal time to positively affirm their good behavior? What about your friend or that business associate? They are faithful, dependable, talented, helpful, fun to be with. You know what they need? Your words of appreciation.

When others speak positive words to us, about us, how should we handle it? We should give them a genuine "thank you" and then pass the compliment on to God. Publicly, when appropriate; privately, always.

Principle #7—Communication with God Involves Confession
"If we confess our sins, He is faithful and righteous to forgive our sins and to cleanse us from all unrighteousness" (1 John 1:9). Along with this classic statement of the need for confession, Psalm 51 and Psalm 32 also deal with the issue. Psalm 32 details the experience of one struggling with unconfessed sin. *"When I kept silent about my sin, my body wasted away through my groaning all day long"* (32:3). He was trying to hide his sin from God. The longer he hid it, the more miserable he became. When he confessed it, he experienced relief and joy (32:1, 2, 5).

When we are listening carefully to God, we will examine our lives and deal with those things that are wrong. Communication brings conviction which leads to confession. Why do we need to confess? Our relationship with God the Father is settled and secure in Jesus Christ. We have positional forgiveness.[8] Our fellowship with God is temporal. Conscious, willfull disobedience breaks fellowship.[9] We need practical forgiveness. Though a disobedient child is not put out of the family by the parents, the parents are most certainly "put out" with him and as a result he is out of fellowship with them. Confession allows him to experience the practical reality of their forgiveness and his restoration to fellowship. So it is with God's children.

The Bible also emphasizes the horizontal implications of confession and forgiveness. The words of the returning prodigal son indicate the importance of both the vertical and the horizontal. *"Father, I have sinned against heaven and in your sight"* (Luke 15:21). Christ also taught His disciples to *"first be reconciled to your brother"* and then bring your offering to God (Matthew 5:24). James exhorted believers to *"confess your sins to one another"* (James 5:16). As the Word of the Lord did its work in the hearts of the young Christians in Ephesus they were *"confessing and disclosing their (sinful) practices"* to one another (Acts 19:18-20).

The reason for the need to care for the person-to-person relationship is that our sinful attitudes and actions nearly always affect others. God is offended by our sin. So are people. The sour, grumpy attitudes hurt one's relationship with his wife. The nagging, faultfinding wife offends her husband. The lying salesman does an injustice to the customer. The ridiculing, rebelling teenager demoralizes his parents. The critical, bitter deacon undermines his pastor. To tell God we are sorry about thinking, feeling and saying these things and not communicating anything to the human person(s) involved is to try and short-circuit the process of confession. Talk to God and man about it.

That raises the subject of forgiveness. When we confess, God forgives. When others confess to us, we forgive. Regardless of how often your brother commits the infraction, when he repents, forgive him (Luke 17:3). The teaching of Colossians 3:13 and Ephesians 4:32 is that we are to be continually forgiving those who treat us wrongly. The word used for "forgiving" is not the typical word (*aphiemi,* to let go, send away) used to develop the biblical doctrine of forgiveness which the believer has in Christ, but is the word *charizomai* which means "to freely bestow a favor on someone." To forgive is to do just that—to freely bestow the favor of our unconditional acceptance of and fellowship with another person.[10].

We don't pronounce judicial forgiveness. Only God does that. We proclaim and provide practical, experiential forgiveness. That is, by our attitude and action we reach out and relate to people without holding a grudge or demanding our pound of flesh. We say "I forgive you" and then we *act* like it.

The New Testament emphasizes both the responsibility to confess to one another and the responsibility to forgive one another. When our attitude and actions have hurt another person, we should assume the responsibility of confessing. When we are the one who has been hurt then we should assume the responsibility of forgiving; even if the other party does not confess. An unforgiving spirit is soundly condemned in Scripture. The Lord Jesus taught that those who seek the forgiveness of God must be forgiving of others. Not that God's forgiveness is based on ours, for in Christ we have already received forgiveness, but that our unwillingness to forgive is sin, and until that sin is taken care of, we won't personally and practically *experience* the forgiveness of God. It is in this light we hear our Lord's words:

> *"For if you forgive men for their transgressions, your heavenly Father will also forgive you. But if you do not forgive men, then your Father will not forgive your transgressions."*[11]

Principle #8—Communication with God Should be Personal and Specific

We are to draw near to the throne of grace in order to receive mercy and grace to help in the time of need (Hebrews 4:15). If prayer is to be utilized *in time of need* then it must be vocalized *in terms of need*. Needs are personal. Needs are specific. Prayer must be both. Philippians 4:6 underscores this.

> *"Be anxious for nothing, but in everything by prayer and supplication with thanksgiving let your requests be made known to God."*

"Be anxious for nothing." This command could be translated "stop being concerned about anything." At first glance this would appear to teach that it is wrong for the believer to ever have any anxiety or concern. Yet Paul uses the same word in Philippians 2:20 to speak of a commendable trait in Timothy. He was one who knew how to be genuinely *concerned* for the welfare of others. Furthermore, the Lord Jesus experienced the anxiety of a troubled soul as He anticipated Judas' betrayal and the suffering of the cross (John 12:27; 13:21), and He was without sin (John 8:29; 2 Corinthians 5:21). This is a plea to handle personal anxiety properly. The temptation is to grit our teeth, repress it and do our best to muddle through. That is precisely what this verse says

we are not to do. Don't let anxiety eat away at you internally. Get it out. Talk it through. Quit trying to handle it on your own. Share it with God.

"In everything." Feel free to talk to God about everything that concerns you. No need to hide anything. Especially the anxieties that go along with interpersonal conflicts (4:2) and situations where you have to put up with less than the ideal (4:5).

"By prayer." This is the first of a number of terms used in this verse to describe the nature of our conversation with God. This word, *prosuche*, is always used in the New Testament of address to God. It emphasizes the general fact of prayer rather than any particular form or content.[12] Something bothering you? First and foremost, talk to God.

"And supplication." This word, *deesis,* is used of specific prayer in concrete situations where someone wants something. Jesus prayed that Peter's faith would be strengthened (Luke 22:32). Paul prayed about his travel plans (Romans 1:10; 1 Thessalonians 3:10). The early church prayed about their need for boldness (Acts 4:31). Prayer, then, is to be addressed to God and is to contain the personal needs that we have or that others have for whom we are praying. We are to be "situational" pray-ers.

"With thanksgiving." Here is that positive factor. Even in the midst of personal anxiety, God wants us to accentuate the positive and tell Him we are thankful not only for the events of our lives but also for our relationship with the God who is in control of the events (1 Thessalonians 5:18; Romans 8:28). Anxiety can make us depressed, gloomy, unhappy, and unthankful persons. God helps us keep in balance.

"Your requests." "Supplication" stresses the fact that we are to talk to God about our personal needs. "Requests" underscores the fact that we are *asking* Him to meet these needs. We are not only talking to Him but also asking help from Him. John uses this same word three times in his confident affirmation of what can happen when we pray in faith—*"And if we know that He hears us in whatever we ask,*

we know that we have the requests which we have asked from Him (1 John 5:15).

Some of our prayers would never meet the standards set up so far in Philippians 4:6. Instead they are superficial, vague, cliche-ridden words, usually given for the benefit of others or to fulfill our religious duty. You don't ask the bank *teller* for a loan. You just pass the time of day with her as she handles your business. You don't just pass the time of day with the bank loan *officer.* You ask him for a loan to meet your specific needs. Let's enlarge our concept of who God is and what He can do.

"Be made known. " Why? If God is omniscient, why do we need to "make known" to Him our problems and needs? Certainly not to let Him in on any secrets. He already knows us. Maybe it is purely for our benefit, then. We reap the therapeutic results of talking it over with God. Undoubtedly, that is true, for when we talk to God, we listen to what we say and learn and profit from the experience. But there is more to it than that.

The believer can and should have a growing relationship with God. It is described with terms such as walking, abiding and fellowship (John 15:1ff; 1 John 1:3, 7). How does the believer develop this relationship? One thing he does is talk to God. That is the way we develop relationships with other human beings, by talking with them. How do we develop *deep, intimate, personal* relationships with others? By talking about the deep, intimate, personal things going on in our lives. See how Philippians 4:6 fits in? As we make known our anxieties—which will involve the more personal aspects of our lives—we will deepen our relationship with Him. He knows what is going on in our lives, yet He wants us to share them with Him, because in so doing our fellowship with Him will grow.

I know many of the things that are going on in my teenager's life as she struggles with her identity, her personality, her studies, her future plans, her friendships. Yet I am a very happy father and the relationship between the two of us grows when she voluntarily chooses to share some of these things with me. God feels the same way.

"To God." Led by the Spirit of God, Paul chooses to use *pros,* the Greek preposition of intimacy, here translated "to." It denotes a face-to-face, intimate personal relationship. John uses it to describe the relationship between the Father and the Son (John 1:1, *"and the Word was with God"*). Paul employs it to describe his anticipated relationship with the Lord in heaven (2 Corinthians 5:8, *"at home with the Lord"*). We are not talking at God—long distance. We are talking *with* Him—in an intimate, personal, face-to-face encounter. Remember Hebrews 4:12, 13? There it was God speaking to us intimately. Now here is the same intimacy as we speak to God.

This verse clearly supports the principle that prayer should be personal and specific. When our prayers are impersonal and general, we fail to comply with the Word; we fail to develop a depth relationship with God; and we can easily carry this impersonal, general conversational pattern into our relationships with other people.

"How are things going?"

"Fine."

That is not true and you know it. You are concerned about your job, your wife's health, your child's rebellious attitude. But like most of us, you are caught up in the syndrome of being "neutrally pleasant" with everyone, especially fellow Christians. God is not satisfied with that level of conversation. As we learn to share more openly and honestly with Him it will be easier and more natural for us to share similarly with others. As we stop hiding from God, we will stop hiding from people.

The solution is not to fill the church's program with the more intimate sharing of "body life" services. Those who aren't sharing intimately with God can be quite threatened at the prospect of sharing intimately with others. Those who aren't accustomed to hearing themselves verbalize honestly to God, will probably be a bit shocked to hear others verbalize honestly to members of the body. A deeper prayer life will help prepare us for real, biblical *koinonia.*

Principle #9—Communication with God Can Bring Immediate, Internal Results

Another way of stating this principle would be: You can get answers to prayer while you are praying. We have just studied Philippians 4:6. It details our responsibilities in prayer. Now look at Philippians 4:7. It gives the results when we fulfill our responsibilities.

> *"And the peace of God, which surpasses all comprehension, shall guard your hearts and your minds in Christ Jesus."*

First, note that the results are *internal.* That's because the problem is internal. Anxiety may well be caused by external issues and individuals, but it is also an internal experience that we are having. We need internal results and that is what God promises—*peace.* A peace that originates with God "surpasses all comprehension," not because it is relatively superior to knowledge, but because it is absolutely unique and beyond the range of our comprehension. It guards us internally—our hearts and minds. The meaning of peace deserves a full, separate treatment not possible here, but let me at least alert the reader to some biblical concepts that need to be considered.

Peace is not the absence of emotions. Christ had peace. But at the same time He also experienced a full range of emotions—anger, joy, sorrow, and a troubled soul.[13] There are two basic factors involved in peace. It comes as a result of *knowing the truth* and applying it in the given situation. Jesus said to troubled disciples: *"These things I have spoken to you, that in Me you may have peace"* (John 16:33). His words of truth gave them peace. To the same troubled disciples He said: *"Let not your heart be troubled; believe in God, believe also in Me"* (John 14:1). *Faith* is the other component which is essential if real peace is to be experienced. So peace comes as a result of knowledge and faith. Since it guards the heart and mind, it must involve truth. Since it surpasses all comprehension, it demands faith. Truth + Trust = Peace.

The same components are seen in James 1:2-8. The believer who is involved in various trials needs to know what is going on and why. Verses 3 and 4 provide insight about these trials. They are to test your faith, produce endurance and bring you to full maturity. If you need additional wisdom to handle the pressure and tension of trials, you know where to get it—ask God (v. 5). And one's attitude is important— *"let him ask in faith without any doubting"* (v. 6). That means that we come to God believing that He is able to give us wisdom and also believing that what is happening in our lives is one of the good things and perfect gifts bestowed from above (v. 17). Peace is not mentioned specifically in this passage, but a similar result is—joy (v. 2). A lack of faith will not only result in a lack of needed wisdom, it will also manifest a lack of composure. Internal doubting will arise, *"like the surf of the sea driven and tossed by the wind"* (v. 6). Such stormy inner feelings are the opposite of peace and joy. Faith and wisdom would calm the inner turmoil.

Second, these internal results can be *immediate.* Fulfill the responsibilities outlined in Philippians 4:6 and you can experience the results of Philippians 4:7. When? I used to think that I should pray for peace and then wait. To pray "in faith" was to pray expecting to wait for the answer. Then our four children came along and I couldn't wait! Reacting to their hairstyles, lifestyles, rebellion, problems and unpredictability was overloading my circuits with internal anxiety. I needed help—quick. It was here in the crucible of those needs that I discovered there is no time gap between Philippians 4:6 and 4:7. If I fulfilled my obligations in verse 6, God would give me the promised peace of verse 7—*even while I was praying.* I had been using verse 6 as a crutch to perpetuate my flaccid faith, instead of a clutch to engage His powerful peace.

Many times, the reason Christians don't have peace is because they haven't really talked to God about the specific, personal details of life and asked Him in faith to give them the wisdom they need to handle the situation peacefully. When I carefully articulate what it is that is bothering me, God will bring His Word to bear on the issue and I will understand. But I will never understand it all, so I must also express the reality of my confidence in God who knows all and does right.

Personal, specific prayer can bring immediate, internal results. We need to pray like this. We need to teach others to pray like this. As we learn to talk to God in this manner, we can talk with others in the same way, when appropriate. Just as God encourages us to be personal and specific with Him, we should encourage others in the body to communicate similarly with us and with each other. When anxious people ask counsel from us, they should get peace—as a result of our communicating the Word of God to them, and as a result of our (and subsequently their) faith in the God of the Word.

The church needs to provide opportunities for people to openly and honestly share with each other what it is they don't understand; what it is that is bothering them. Yet the greater portion of the program of the average local church is designed for the many to listen to the few. God says: "Talk to Me and to each other, openly and honestly, and you will find wisdom and peace." The church often says: "Listen to the pastor and the Sunday School teacher and you will find wisdom and peace." People are looking for instant insight and short cuts to serenity. Peace without openness. Wisdom without honesty. Fellowship without intimacy. There isn't any.

In Summary

We have explored the meaning and implications of nine principles relating to how we communicate with God.

1. Communication with God Involves the Holy Spirit.
2. Communication with God Involves Man as an Active Participant.
3. I Can Always Have God's Undivided Attention.
4. I Can't Hide Anything from God.
5. I Can Tell God Everything.
6. Communication with God Always Involves the Positive.
7. Communication with God Involves Confession.
8. Communication with God Should be Personal and Specific.
9. Communication with God Can Bring Immediate, Internal Results.

Interaction

1. "Always pray about a matter before you talk to anyone else about it." Is this a commitment that you think Christians ought to make? Why? Why not?

2. Why is it difficult to give people our undivided attention?

3. What are some of the typical phrases you and others use in your prayers? How might we say the same thing in different words?

4. In private prayer do you pray out loud or silently? Why?

5. What are some of the typical phrases we use in casual conversation with others? What purpose do they serve?

6. How honest should we be when someone asks us how things are going?

Footnotes

[1]A. T. Robertson, *A Grammar of the Greek New Testament in the Light of Historical Research* (Nashville: Broadman Press, 1934), p. 573.

[2]Psalm 66:18; Proverbs 15:29; Isaiah 1:15.

[3]Exodus 2:24; 2 Chronicles 33:10-13.

[4]Psalm 50:14; 23; Ephesians 5:20; Philippians 4:6; Colossians 4:2; Mark 14:23; Luke 17:11-19; Psalm 103:1-5; Hebrews 13:14; 1 Thessalonians 5:18.

[5]Luke 11:2; Matthew 6:9; 1 Timothy 1:7; Jude 24-25; Psalm 100.

[6]Romans 1:8; 1 Corinthians 1:4; Ephesians 1:16; Philippians 1:3; Colossians 1:3; 1 Thessalonians 1:3.

[7]Galatians 1:6; 1 Corinthians 1:10.

[8]Ephesians 1:7; Colossians 1:14; 1 John 2:12; Romans 8:1.

[9]1 John 1:1-10; John 15:1-14; Acts 8:22; James 5:15; Psalm 32:1, 5.

[10]For the other similar uses of this word in the New Testament see 2 Corinthians 2:7, 10; 12:13; Colossians 2:13; Luke 7:42-43.

[11]Matthew 6:14-15; cf. Matthew 6:12-14; 18:21-35; Mark 11:25; Luke 11:4.

[12]Acts 6:4; Romans 12:12; Ephesians 6:18.

[13]Mark 3:1-5; Luke 10:21; John 11:35; 12:27.

Resources

1. For insight on prayer: *How To Talk With God* by Stephen Winward, Harold Shaw Publishers, 1973, and *Praying Jesus' Way* by Curtis C. Mitchell, Fleming H. Revell Company, 1977.

2. For insight on becoming a more open communicator: *Secrets* by Paul Tournier, John Knox Press, 1965, and *Why Am I Afraid to Tell You Who I Am?* by John Powell, Argus Communications, 1969.

Chapter 8

Communicating with Yourself

I enjoy mowing the lawn. Not just to make the yard look better, but to have an opportunity to talk to myself. Mowing doesn't require much concentration and the roar of the motor gives me the privacy I need. The front and back yards have been the setting for numerous internal dialogues. I do it when I'm shaving, driving to work, sitting on the back porch, studying in my office or jogging. I do it silently. I do it out loud. I work on problems, set goals, make plans, test alternatives, and talk to people who aren't there. During my college days I worked two summers on a cattle ranch and farm in northern Arizona. A lot of my time was spent riding a horse, driving a tractor and irrigating fields. I can still remember some of the long, illuminating conversations I had with myself!

We all do it. We all talk to ourselves numerous times during the day. When we are with others we can carry on silently, though there are times when we become so excited or upset that we may blurt out our inner thoughts. When we are alone, we often vocalize to ourselves. Children do it all the time. How often have you paused outside the room to listen to a child carrying on an animated conversation with himself

141

or an imaginary playmate? We never grow out of it. Even adults need to talk to themselves.

Our Natural Tendency—Self-Deception

We have already seen that as sinners we are self-centered communicators. We are also *self-deceptive* persons, and therefore, self-deceptive communicators. *"The heart,"* said the prophet Jeremiah, *"is more deceitful than all else"* (17:9). *"Out of the heart of man proceeds...deceit,"* said Christ (Mark 7:22). This causes Solomon to state that *"the way of a fool is right in his own sight"* (Proverbs 12:15). Even as Christians we are self-styled con-artists and we start by fooling ourslves. We have plenty of encouragement, for Satan *"is a liar, and the father of lies"* (John 8:44), and he is avidly seeking to get us to conform to that kind of false communication pattern. If the great deceiver can get us to lie to ourselves, he has us inwardly conforming to his system.

How do we deceive ourselves? One way is by thinking more highly of ourselves than we ought to think (Romans 12:3). We can tell ourselves we are really something great when the truth is—we aren't. We are imperfect and immature—just like everybody else. Or we can transmit a message to ourselves that we are nothing, a big fat zero, when the truth is that we are gifted and able to serve God and do His will. The latter opinion is the kind of "sound judgment" we are to give to ourselves (Romans 12:3). We may know some of these truths but deceptively hide them and not give them our full consideration.

Timothy seemed to have such a problem. He was a timid young man who was thrust into a position of leadership. He apparently had let himself drift into thinking that he didn't really have what it would take to do the job. He didn't quit, but obviously he wasn't functioning at a high performance level, for Paul came down hard on his deceptive inferiority thinking. He told him not to allow people to look down on his youthfulness; to realize that with the Holy Spirit he had power; and that instead of fading into the woodwork he was to get out in front and be a prime example of one who could lead and live confidently (1 Timothy 4:12; 2 Timothy 1:7).

It is also deceptive thinking that causes us to wrongly compare ourselves with others (2 Corinthians 10:12). It is deceptive thinking that causes us to come to conclusions on the basis of outward appearance (John 7:24; 1 Samuel 16:17). It is deceptive thinking that causes us to assume that we can get away with it—to convince ourselves that we won't always reap what we sow (Galatians 6:7, 8). It is deceptive to tell ourselves that the wisdom of the world is enough; we don't really need Christ and the wisdom of God (Colossians 2:8; 1 Corinthians 3:18, 19). We deceive ourselves when we operate on the premise that charm and beauty give us the status we want (Proverbs 31:30). We deceive ourselves when we become convinced that we can give equal billing in our lives to material possessions *and* God. Christ said it wouldn't work (Mark 4:19; Matthew 13:22). We deceive ourselves by gauging our spirituality on religious activity. For, even though we worship regularly, if we are saying unkind, untrue words to or about another we are prime candidates for the hypocrite club (James 1:26). To believe that it is more important to hear the Word than to do it, is to deceive oneself (James 1:22). To believe that one can claim to be saved and yet habitually engage in sin is to be deceived (1 Corinthians 6:9; cf. 1 John 1:8, 3:7). To think that we can run around with the wrong crowd without being negatively influenced is deception (1 Corinthians 15:33). To blame God or anyone but ourselves for committing an act of sin is thoroughly deceitful (James 1:13-17).

Paul summarizes it well by stating that the individual who is mature will not be susceptible to *"deceitful scheming"* (Ephesians 4:14). Though the passage deals with the deceitful schemes foisted on us by others, maturity will enable us to handle deception, whether from others or from ourselves.

The preceding has been a survey of some of the teaching of the Word of God on the subject of self-deception. We could expand it biblically, for there is much more. We could expand it practically, too. And we shall.

Here are some statements we might make to ourselves, about ourselves, and about others. Analyze each one. In what sense could each statement be true? In what sense could each statement involve self-deception?

"I couldn't help it."
"It was all her fault."
"I can't do anything right."
"I want everybody to like me."
"I can handle this problem by myself."
"I want to be totally independent."
"I did the best I could."
"I don't have anything worthwhile to say."
"I could have done a better job than that."
"It was all my fault."
"They don't appreciate me."

Do you want to go further with your analysis? Okay. Which of the above statements could involve rationalization? (The process of justifying our behavior.) Projection? (Seeing your faults in others.) Repression? (Forgetting the unpleasant.) We all have an array of psychic armor we can put on to protect our ego. When we use it, in one way or another, we deceive ourselves. Our natural tendency is toward self-deception. We don't always lie to ourselves. But neither do we always tell ourselves the truth.

The following diagram will help us grasp the concept. When we are in the inner circle we are centered on the Word and saying the right things to ourselves. We are not thinking too highly of ourselves, nor are we depreciating the value we have in God's sight and the potential we have in God's service. We are carrying on an internal dialogue that is doctrinally accurate and therefore practically profitable.

Our tendency is to get out of the inner circle and think too high or too low. In either case we are not telling ourselves the truth. In both cases we are deceiving ourselves. By the way, let's be candidly honest about the fact that none of us,

no matter how long we have walked with the Lord, ever gets permanently situated in the inner circle. We are all vulnerable and we are vulnerable all the time. You can have a healthy self-concept and still talk yourself right out of the inner circle when things don't go as you planned, when you are praised for being successful or when you are criticized for being a failure. *"Let him who thinks he stands take heed lest he fall"* (1 Corinthians 10:12).

Our Resources for Right Self-Thinking

The Word. It is able to judge the thoughts and intentions of our heart (Hebrews 4:12). It is designed to teach, reprove, correct and train us so that we will be adequately equipped to deal with ourselves (2 Timothy 3:16, 17). It renews my mind so that I can (internally) decide what the will of God is (Romans 12:2).

When I dwell on a problem in one of my children's lives, the Word helps me focus on the real issue and helps me determine how I may have contributed to the problem and can contribute to the solution. For example, a father is not to provoke his child to anger (Ephesians 6:4). In a Word-oriented internal dialogue, I might come to the conclusion that my provocation was the real problem, and then go on to solve it on that basis.

Visualize the football coach on the sidelines. While he is deciding what play to run or what player to send in, he is getting insight through his earphones from the spotters high above. Insight that helps him think it through and act. In the same manner, while you are talking to yourself; you can also be listening to God. Provided you know the Word.

Prayer. Through it we can verbalize our thoughts and feelings. Our anxieties and aspirations. Technically speaking, the Christian never really talks only to himself. The Lord is always there. Always listening. We usually separate inner meditation from prayer to God. We do this to emphasize that when we pray, we are talking to God, not ourselves. When we meditate, we are talking to ourselves, not God. But, realistically, you can't talk with God without listening to what you say. In a sense, you are also talking to yourself. And, realistically, you can't talk with yourself without God listening in. You are also talking to Him.

David realized this and said that he wanted the *meditation* of his heart to be acceptable in *God's* sight (Psalm 19:14). Paul in Romans 9:1-5 unveils his inner thoughts and feelings about his unsaved Jewish brethren. With whom is he sharing these thoughts? With the believers in Rome. But note that he also puts an "Amen" at the end of verse 5, as if to say, "I'm sharing this with you *and* with God at the same time." The same combination is seen in Romans 10:1: *"Brethren, my heart's desire and my prayer to God for them is for their salvation.''* He informs people in Rome that he is *meditating* and *praying* about the same thing. Meditation and prayer are not mutually exclusive. Each has its distinctives, but they can and should mutually support and reinforce each other.

Conscience. Within each of us there is the innate and intuitive capacity to distinguish between right and wrong. All of us have moral values written into our hearts and a conscience bearing witness to whether we are adhering to those values or violating them (Romans 2:14, 15). This voice within us will monitor what we say to ourselves.

> "I don't like the way she dresses," you say to yourself.
>
> "She dresses differently, but is it wrong?" replies your conscience. "Is your evaluation based on personal prejudice or biblical standards? If you don't like the dress, what about the person in the dress; do you like her?"

Ideally, the conscience should give us an accurate, Word-centered analysis of what goes on inside us. However, sin has affected even the conscience, and it doesn't always function with precision. It may be too strict or too lenient. It may be too sensitive or calloused (cf. Romans 14; 1 Corinthians 8; 1 Timothy 4:2). The key is to keep renewing the mind with the Word of God, for the weak conscience is the one that does not have adequate, accurate knowledge.

Others. When others talk, we listen. As we listen, we talk to ourselves. We say to ourselves, "I didn't know that." "That's not the way it goes." "I should have done the same thing." Listening becomes silent speech that aids our interior dialogue.

When we talk, others listen. So do we. We listen to ourselves talk. We comment internally on our external conversation. "I believe I got my point across." "He doesn't understand." "I talked too long." "After listening to myself explain it to them, I think I am beginning to understand it."

I am a teacher. My students really contribute to the learning process in my life. When I talk to them, I listen to myself and learn. When they ask questions, I listen to my answers and learn. Sometimes, I learn that I don't know the answers. When they respond in class, I listen to them and learn. I learn in the privacy of my office as I prepare and review.

As a teacher, I can deceive myself. I can convince myself that material is important. My students can help me conclude otherwise. I can be certain that I have a logical, clear presentation to make. Thirty-five confused looks, hands waving in the air and questions galore tell me otherwise.

That's what the church is all about. People relating externally to one another to facilitate internal communication and growth. *"Speaking the truth in love, we are to grow up in all aspects into Him,"* and this happens because of the *"proper working of each individual part"* (Ephesians 4:15, 16). God gives us others to help us think accurately and honestly; to help us stop deceiving ourselves; to help us say the right things, in the right way, at the right time—to ourselves.

On our own, we tend to deceive ourselves. Here's Deluded Don.

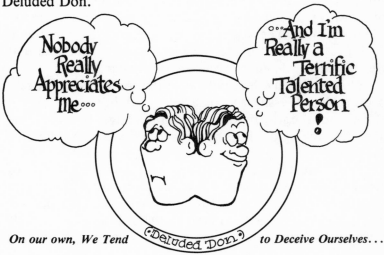

On our own, We Tend *Deluded Don* *to Deceive Ourselves...*

But people do appreciate him. And—he may not be as terrific as he thinks. The beauty of it is, Don doesn't have to operate in a vacuum where all he does is draw erroneous conclusions.

He and all of us have these God-given resources to help us.

. . .but God has given us sources of Truth

The *Holy Spirit* is the divine agent and catalyst in all of these aids. He illuminates the Word; He helps us pray; He instructs our conscience; He works in and through those who listen and talk to us. Resident within us, He helps us filter out the deceptive thinking and filter in the truth that we need to hear and speak.

Our Biblical Responsibilities

Does the Word give us guidelines about what should be on our inner agenda? Yes it does. Here are some of them.

Examine your spiritual position. Look at what Paul wrote to the Corinthians:

> *"Test yourselves to see if you are in the faith; examine yourselves! Or do you not recognize this about yourselves, that Jesus Christ is in you—unless indeed you fail the test?"*
> (2 Corinthians 13:5).

Their lifestyle wasn't all that it could have been, and so Paul exhorts them to start with the basics—*make sure you are really a Christian.* Good advice for anyone. Periodically check your spiritual credentials. Ask yourself if you are really a born-again Christian, and then listen for the Spirit's positive answer, bearing witness with your spirit that you are a child of God (Romans 8:16). At the top of the agenda, talk to yourself about your spiritual position. Are you saved? Are you sure? On what basis? I fly a lot. I review my spiritual position every time the plane takes off!

It is easy to deceive yourself in this realm. You can tell yourself that you are a church member, that you have been baptized and confirmed, that you attend worship services regularly, that you give money to the church, and that you are basically a good person—and because all of these things are true in your life, you can con yourself into thinking that you are a Christian. A Christian is an individual who has a relationship with God through Jesus Christ. Don't settle for anything different; don't settle for anything less. You can be certain that God won't.

Examine your spiritual condition. A number of Scriptures underscore this guideline.

> *"But let a man examine himself, and so let him eat of the bread and drink of the cup"* (1 Corinthians 11:28).

Here is an exhortation to carry on a honest, personal self-examination before participating in the communion service.

"Therefore I do not run like a man running aimlessly; I do not fight like a man beating the air" (1 Corinthians 9:26 NIV). Talk to yourself about your personal goals and how you go about achieving them. What am I living for? What am I working for? How efficient and effective am I? The apostle is telling us that he investigated how he competed and made sure his efforts were aimed carefully and consistently at legitimate goals. Are you a goal-oriented person, or are you just muddling through life? Talk to yourself about that!

> *"You hyprocrite, first take the log out of your own eye; and then you will see clearly enough to take the speck out of your brother's eye"* (Matthew 7:5).

Before you talk to someone else about his problem, talk to yourself first about your own problem. The prerequisite for examining others is to have already successfully examined yourself. It is so easy to talk to yourself about Jane's problem or Bill's attitude and fail to confront yourself with your own problems and attitudes. Do it. It will give you greater credibility with others and greater capability in helping them.

> *"If anyone thinks he is something when he is nothing, he deceives himself. Each one should test his own actions. Then he can take pride in himself, without comparing himself to somebody else."* (Galatians 6:3, 4 NIV).

Be careful what you tell yourself about yourself. To pat yourself on the back when you need to kick yourself elsewhere is to deceive yourself. Examine carefully who you are, what you have, what you have done and can do and on that basis draw your conclusions about your position and potential. Don't compare yourself with others. You can always find somebody below you. Compare yourself with God's standards. You may well conclude that by His help there are areas where you are becoming what He wants you to become. You are making spiritual progress. You can take pride in that, recognizing that all that you are and have is of God.

Talk to yourself about your spiritual position and your spiritual condition and you will communicate on all of the really important issues of life. Do it using the resources of the Holy Spirit, the Word, prayer, conscience and others and you will avoid self-deception and speak the truth to yourself.

A Word of Caution about Introspection

No one ever gets a great idea without someone else carrying it too far. If a little introspection is good; then a lot must be better. Not necessarily so. We are prone to magnify our miseries. Wallow in our worries. To dwell almost morbidly on certain issues and events. We can do this for hours, days, weeks, even months and years. This is not healthy, nor is it biblical. The same Bible that motivates us to internal investigation also tells us that the general tenor of our thought life is to be *positive*.

> *"Finally, brethren, whatever is true, whatever is honorable, whatever is right, whatever is pure, whatever is lovely, whatever is of good repute, if there is any excellence and if anything worthy of praise, let your mind dwell on these things"* (Philippians 4:8).

Positive thinking is to be a habit of life for the believer. In 1 Corinthians 13:5 Paul says that love *"does not take into account a wrong suffered."* This means that the loving person will not allow himself to dwell on the fact that he may have been misunderstood, misrepresented or wrongfully treated. Another way of dealing with the whole subject is Paul's admonition to take *"every thought captive to the obedience of Christ"* (2 Corinthians 10:5). The Bible leaves no room for morbid, depressing, gloomy introspection.

The next verse in Philippians 4 adds another balancing factor.

"The things you have learned and received and heard and seen in me, practice these things; and the God of peace shall be with you" (v. 9).

Self-examination is imperative and important. But that is not the only way we grow. We must continue to relate to people. The overly introspective person often tends to withdraw from healthy interpersonal relationships. Yet this verse presupposes that the Philippians had dynamic relationships with Paul, and teaches us that we should have similar meaningful relationships with other believers. Watch their example. Learn from them. There is no place in Scripture for a secluded, isolated, self-absorbed Christian. Communication is always to be a balance of the *intra*personal and the *inter*personal. We are to think positive *and* relate to people.

Furthermore, the words we speak to others and ourselves are to *edify*. Morbid introspection does not edify. Paul shared some sober, soul-searching words with the Corinthians. Yet, his overall evaluation of these words was that it was *"all for your upbuilding, beloved"* (2 Corinthians 12:19; cf. 13:10). We may speak the same kind of words to ourselves but not ultimately to depress and defeat and demoralize, but to edify, to promote personal growth.

Some Practical Observations

Our *way of life* militates against consistent, careful, healthy introspection. We are too busy. Too distracted. Too bombarded by various media. Too involved in work. Too engaged in recreation. Too wrapped up in entertainment. Too tired. Radio, television, newspapers, magazines, books, billboards, movies, tape recorders, record players and telephones—helpful as they may be—rob us of the opportunity to do some fruitful pondering. Along with all the rights that are being defended today, someone needs to lobby for the "right to reflect."

I am so caught up in this rat race that I usually load up a briefcase full of books to read during my vacation taken for the purpose of "getting away from the books." Undisturbed brooding is so foreign to our lifestyle that we almost feel guilty—at least, unproductive—when we engage in it.

Read the psalms. Are they the product of harried authors who put a lot of stuffy facts together quickly in order to meet the divine editor's deadline? Hardly. Many of them are the obvious product of reflective thinking. Look at Psalm 19. The first part (vv. 1-6) was probably composed by David while he was flat on his back! Not because he was sick, but because he was pensively gazing at the skies above. He wasn't preparing for tomorrow's astronomy class. He was simply, yet profoundly, communing with himself about the immensity and uniqueness of the created celestial universe. The Spirit led him to write it down for us to read. In verses 7-11 he isn't rattling off his bibliology notes. He is reflecting on the effect the Word of God was having in his life and in the lives of others. In verses 12-14 he brings God into his inner soliloquy. With God he shares his needs (vv. 12, 13) and his commitment (v. 14). The entire psalm was conceived and nurtured in the mind of a meditator, who incidently was a very busy man.

Look at Psalm 42:5.

> *"Why are you in despair, O my soul?*
> *And why have you become disturbed with me?*
> *Hope in God, for I shall again praise Him*
> *For the help of His presence."*

The writer is talking to God in the verses preceding and following, but in this verse *he is talking to himself* (cf. 42:11; 43:5). He is communicating with his despairing, disturbed soul. First he probes himself with questions: *"Why are you in despair... why have you become disturbed?"* Then he offers himself succinct counsel: *"Hope in God."* Finally, he predicts to and for himself that he will definitely be able to praise God for the help He is going to give him. When you talk to yourself, *tell yourself the right things!* Carve some time out of your own busy schedule. Get away from all distractions and interruptions. Then talk to yourself.

The *world* we live in doesn't help matters. The philosophy of our day is to mass produce human beings. To decide on a good pattern and cut everybody out to fit that pattern. So we tend to get our cues from outside ourselves. We tend to thoughtlessly adapt to the majority and to mindlessly adopt a secular viewpoint and lifestyle. All of this militates against exploring and developing our inner selves. Don't let the world conform you to this "other directed" approach to life and growth (Romans 12:2). Take time to become *"fully convinced in your own mind"* as to what is right and wrong and what you intend to be and do as a person (Romans 14:5). Program into your personal calendar *intra*personal interaction sessions wherein you *"examine everything carefully; hold fast to that which is good; abstain from every form of evil"* (1 Thessalonians 5:21, 22).

The *church* can and should play a positive role in facilitating internal investigation. Along with programs that help us learn and serve, the church should encourage and equip believers in the art of soul-searching. The concepts we have dealt with in this chapter need to be shared with people. Opportunities to talk about them and to try them out should be provided.

For example, *retreats* are great for getting away to do some profitable pondering. By all means don't fill the retreat program with too many meetings and planned activities. Provide blocks of unstructured time when people can wander off and talk to themselves and God. Our orientation toward structured sessions may cause us to feel like this is wasting time; but if believers have been taught the biblical importance of communicating with themselves, they will regard it as an opportunity to redeem the time.

Sermons and Sunday School *lessons* are often so loaded with facts that the audience or class doesn't have time to really think about the material being presented. Maybe it would help if once in a while the speaker paused and said, "Let me take a moment to tell you what I think about what I am saying." He could then proceed to let his listeners in on some of his own honest reflective thinking about the truth being studied. Has it been easy to understand? Easy to accept as true? Easy to apply to life? How do you feel about it? Excited? Apathetic? Motivated? Worried? Of course, if all you have done is mastered a set of facts, then you won't have much to share in the realm of personal, reflective thinking. But if the truth is being digested and assimilated into your spiritual bloodstream and you report on this process, it will stimulate others to compare their inner thoughts with yours and prompt some to go beyond passive listening to active mulling. Then the leader might ask the audience to share what *they* are thinking about the subject at hand. Every Sunday a wealth of reflective thinking remains untapped in evangelical churches.

A Biblical Example

Peter had been doing a lot of thinking—to himself. He had watched Jesus perform miracles. He had listened to His authoritative words. He was ready to respond when Jesus posed the question to the disciples that day in Caesarea Philippi (Matthew 16:15).

> Jesus: *"Who do you say that I am?"*
> Peter: *"Thou art the Christ, the Son of the living God."*

Jesus then went on to commend Peter for what he had said and to predict a significant ministry for him. What thoughts were welling up in Peter's mind at that point? The same kind that well up within you when someone asks you a question, and you give the right answer and they lavish praise on you. You are sorely tempted to entertain thoughts that are proud and self-centered. Peter was enjoying a moment of success. Success always has the potential to create improper internal dialogue. Success can easily lead to self-deception. It is so comfortable to bask in the warm rays of praise. Watch out—you can get burned. While Peter meditated on his own magnificence the Lord went on

> *"to show His disciples that He must go to Jerusalem, and suffer many things from the elders and chief priests and scribes, and be killed, and be raised up on the third day"* (Matthew 16:21).

As Peter listened to these sobering words he thought to himself something like this:

> I'm a pretty sharp fellow. I know what's going on. Didn't I come through with the right answer to the Lord's question? Sure I did. Didn't He commend me for my insight? Sure he did. Well, then, I need to step in here and help the Lord. He's talking about suffering, death and resurrection. He's got it all wrong. That couldn't happen to him. He's not making sense. Somebody needs to talk to Him right now, and I'm the one to do it.

So Peter took Him aside and began to rebuke Him, saying, *"God forbid it, Lord! This shall never happen to You"* (Matthew 16:22). When you are convinced you know *something,* it is easy to think that you know *everything!* That is exactly what happened to Peter. Having successfully determined who Jesus was, he succumbed to the subtle temptation to determine what Jesus would do. He was talking when he should have been listening.

Jesus interrupts Peter's forthright words with His own candid comment: *"Get behind Me, Satan! You are a stumbling-block to Me; for you are not setting your mind on God's interests, but man's"* (Matthew 16:23). Now Peter had something else to think about. These words knocked him off his pedestal and fractured his ego—causing him to reflect soberly. "Satan . . . stumbling block . . . not God's interests—all of that true—about me?" Though probably a private conversation, still an embarrassing moment for Peter.

Embarrassment can be healthy, because it can make us face facts—about ourselves. At this point I would imagine that Peter engaged himself in a serious session of contemplative thinking. He might have said something like this:

> What did I say wrong? I thought I was right on track—helping the Lord out. The way He came back at me. Boy, I must have really blown it. I have to figure this out. Now let's see . . .

That would have been healthy introspection. Unhealthy introspection would have been to get mad at the Lord and defend himself or to decide he was a failure and quit. Whatever direction his inner musings took, they were helped by the Lord's next words on discipleship (Matthew 16:24-28). *"If anyone wishes to come after Me, let him deny himself, and take up his cross and follow Me. For whoever wishes to save his life shall lose it; but whoever loses his life for My sake shall find it"* (Matthew 16:24-25).

> Ah—now I see. I was trying to lead the Lord. I need to follow Him. I was trying to take down the Lord's cross. I need to take up my cross. I was trying to direct the Lord. I need to deny myself. I was trying to work on my reputation. I need to be willing to lose it.

It was one of the low points in Peter's life. That night he probably told himself he was a big-mouthed failure. Could have been one of the most intelligent things he said all day.

Peter had other experiences like this. Convinced of the sincerity of his devout dedication and not too sensitive to his weaknesses he said, *"even though all may fall away because of You, I will never fall away . . . even if I must die with You, I will not deny You"* (Matthew 26:33, 35). When you think there is a sin that you cannot commit, you are deceiving yourself. Jesus told Peter that he would deny Him three times. He did just that and then *"went out and wept bitterly"*(Matthew 26:75). That put Peter at the bottom. He experienced the agony of loneliness, misery and humiliation. He knew enough truth to engage in some healthy introspection. He was also low enough to do some unhealthy thinking. The Lord knew where he was and what he needed. He spent some quality time with Peter after the resurrection (John 20:15-23). The next time we see Peter, he is preaching confidently to thousands at Pentecost (Acts 2). One of the reasons why he was able to say the right things to all those people was that he had been saying the right things to himself.

Peter's problem of self-deception was just like yours and mine: a nagging tendency to think more highly of himself than he ought to think. God allowed circumstances to occur that brought him low. In those low moments he began to see in himself and say to himself the things that needed to be seen and said. Here was a man who was eminently qualified to write to others: *"Humble yourselves, therefore, under the mighty hand of God, that He may exalt you at the proper time"* (1 Peter 5:6). He had tried exalting himself. Now he was content to let God do it.

In Summary

The Scriptures encourage self-communication. The primary purpose of this inward look is for *evaluation*. Note how frequently the words *examine* and *test* occurred in the passages we studied. That makes sense, because our tendency is to hide and hurl. Our need, then, is to examine what we are keeping to ourselves and what we are communicating to others. Self-communication is not just to pass the time of day; it is to probe deeply into our inner selves, discover our needs and apply God's truth. This won't happen unless we communicate openly, honestly and appropriately with our own selves.

We all have an offstage (or backstage) life and an onstage life. The offstage life is the private realm where we think, plan, rehearse, review, repent and evaluate. The onstage life is where we perform—according to the role(s) we have decided on and developed offstage. This chapter has focused on the offstage life. It is crucial to the onstage life. How do we know what to do offstage in order to prepare for the onstage drama of life? Very simple. Read, study, memorize and be mastered by—the *script*. Talk to yourself. Examine yourself. Let all your internal dialogue be governed by the Word. Then, whenever and wherever you step on the stage, you will play the role God wants you to play—according to the *Scrip-ture*.

"The spirit of man is the lamp of the Lord, searching all the innermost parts of his being" (Proverbs 20:27). God has endowed us with this wonderful capacity of self-consciousness. We can know ourselves. We can examine ourselves. We can talk to ourselves. And we can deceive ourselves. Our responsibility is to carry on a consistent, Word-oriented, Spirit-directed, soul-searching conversation with ourselves.

Interaction

1. Here are some more biblical examples of introspection. You may wish to study and discuss them. What caused the introspection? Is it healthy or unhealthy? If unhealthy, what should have been said?
   * Elijah—I Kings 19:1-21
   * Paul—Acts 26:9; Romans 7:14-25
   * Nebuchadnezzar—Daniel 4:28-37
   * Pharisee—Luke 18:11, 12
   * Prodigal son—Luke 15:17-19
   * Isaiah—Isaiah 6:5

2. "Nothing requires a rarer intellectual heroism than willingness to see one's equation written out." What does this mean? How does it relate to the concepts presented in this chapter?

3. What are some of the areas where you tend to deceive yourself? Why?

4. Are there certain times when you tend to be more introspective? Why? Are there particular topics about which you tend to be more introspective? Why?

5. In teaching this chapter, be sure your class understands the problems of self-deception, introspection and busyness, and their biblical responsibility to engage in healthy reflective thinking. Encourage people to share insights from their own experience of self-communication and to set some personal goals in this important area of personal meditation.

Resources

1. For insight on self-image: *The Christian Looks at Himself* by Anthony Hoekema, Eerdmans, 1975; *The Sensation of Being Somebody* by Maurice Wagner, Zondervan, 1975; and *Search For Identity* by Earl Jabay, Zondervan, 1967.

2. For insight on emotions: *How To Live With Your Feelings* by Phillip J. Swihart, InterVarsity Press, 1976.

3. For insight on the conscience: *Knowing God's Will—And Doing It* by J. Grant Howard, Jr., Zondervan, 1976, ch. 9.

Chapter 9

Communicating with Others

*L*et's review the problem: we hide and hurl because we are self-centered individuals. We need a relationship with someone from whom we can't hide, at whom we can hurl, and who will always tell us the truth. God meets these qualifications. In Christ we can have such a relationship: one wherein we listen to God in His Word and talk to God in prayer. This gives us the pattern and the power to communicate with ourselves and with others. In this chapter we will focus explicitly on communicating with others.

Why Don't We?

We don't always communicate well with others. Why not? We have already dealt with the *theological factors.* We are self-centered sinners who tend to hide and hurl. This is a simple statement of a complex issue. We need to examine other contributing factors.

Educational factors. Many of us are the product of a knowledge-oriented educational system using methodology that majored on one-way communication—talking teachers and listening students. This has subtly but powerfully affected our communication patterns. For the most part, the

163

church's educational system is no different from the public system. Education tends to make us passive listeners, rather than active thinkers and talkers. A knowledge-oriented curriculum tends to stress what we know. A curriculum based on knowledge *plus* obedience and competency would, of necessity, demand more active, involved communication to and from the students.

Historical factors. At the turn of the century, liberal theologians began to question the inspired, authoritative Scriptures and began to champion human reason, human potential, human needs and human relationships. Sin was seen primarily as an environmental problem. Hence the rise of the social gospel. Conservative Christians rightly countered by stressing the inspired, authoritative Scriptures and the total depravity of man, and consequently tended to put less emphasis on the personal, interpersonal and societal. The emphasis was solidly on the communication of propositional truth to rescue and renew man. Receiving less emphasis were the people involved and the process of sending and receiving the message. This conservative counteraction to liberalism can be diagrammed in this way:

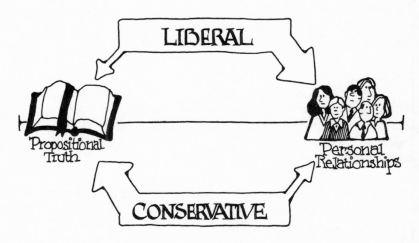

Conservative Christians did not emphasize Companionship

As a result, the conservative Christian community was more oriented around content than companionship, doctrine than fellowship, intake than interaction, studying than sharing.

Things are definitely changing, though. In the past fifteen years there has been a healthy move toward stressing both propositional truth *and* personal relationships. "Body life" and "growth groups" are evidences of this healthy, balancing trend. We need to continue to work on achieving and maintaining this balance and to be constantly vigilant lest we get out of balance—either way.

Sociological factors. Thirty-six million Americans— nearly a fifth of all U.S. families—change their residences every year. High *mobility* and intimate friendships are antipathetic. People who move a lot don't develop close personal relationships.

This is an age of *specialization*. People have less in common occupationally. Fewer natural bridges for communication. Occupational diversity can cause a lot of people to be satisfied with "small talk." Thirty years ago most of the adult members of a congregation were farmers, merchants or housewives. Today you will find an engineer who designs integrated circuits for hand-held computers worshipping next to an educator who specializes in reading disabilities in first graders. Their worlds are so different they tend to bridge the gap with a brief "Hi, how are you."

We enjoy *isolation*. After a day's work in a busy, message-centered world, people want to go home and be by themselves. After a week of work in a world teeming with people, we want a weekend of privacy. So we build fences, mountain cabins, buy boats and campers, take trips—anything to get away from it all. Isolation doesn't always foster communication.

We are *spectators*. A nation of non-involved watchers. We sit at home and watch television. We buy tickets and go and sit with thousands of others (whom we don't know) and watch professionals perform. We go to church and sit with others (whom we know superficially) and watch religious professionals perform. Admission is free but an offering is taken which gives the spectators an opportunity to express appreciation for and approval of a good performance. Even Christians are afflicted with spectatoritis. Onlookers aren't usually working on communication skills.

We are caught up in the *throwaway* syndrome. Everything is disposable, why not relationships? So—just as we use a Kleenex, wad it up and throw it away—we smile, exchange a handshake and greeting, say goodby and walk away. We have neither the time nor the interest to develop deep, lasting relationships with anything or anybody.

We lack *intergenerational* interaction. The nuclear family (Dad, Mom and the kids) is the basic unity of society. Senior citizens retire and live in their specially designed communities. Churches perpetuate this by planning very few things that cause young and old to study, pray, fellowship and serve together. Titus 2:1-8 teaches us that the older have something to say to the younger. 1 Timothy 4:12 teaches us that the younger have something to say to the older.

There is a temptation for Christians to regard themselves as immune to the adverse effects of these theological, educational, historical and sociological factors. We are not. We are just as susceptible to being conformed to the world we live in as anyone else. At the same time, we are responsible to be different—to be transformed people—people who communicate with others openly, honestly and appropriately, in spite of the world's pressure to do otherwise.

The Scriptures are replete with data about how, what and why believers are to communicate with others. In this section we will survey some of the significant material. Suggestions for further study will be given at the end of the chapter. Don't forget, also, that we have already said much about the subject in chapters six and seven, where we developed many of the horizontal implications of our vertical communication with God.

The Basic Nature of our Communication with Others

Nonverbal communication. God does it. He communicates nonverbally through the created universe, through God-made things like the plagues and the flood, through man-made things like the tabernacle and the Babylonian captivity. The Scriptures also have something to say about the nonverbal communication of believers. We are to let the world *see* our good works (Matthew 5:17). We are to abstain from every *appearance* of evil (1 Thessalonians 5:22). A woman's clothing (or lack of it) communicates a message and therefore women are to dress modestly and discreetly (1 Timothy 2:9). The acts of eating the bread and drinking of the cup are silent proclamations of truth about the Lord's death (1 Corinthians 11:26).

"Body language" is not a 20th-century phenomenon. The Bible talks about it. The "right hand of fellowship" from James, Cephas and John communicated approval of Paul and Barnabas and their ministry to the Gentiles (Galatians 2:9). Greeting one another with a holy kiss was a meaningful way of expressing concern for others (1 Corinthians 16:20). The look that Christ gave Peter spoke powerfully though silently (Luke 22:61). The act of washing another's feet says something concrete about servanthood (John 13:1-18). Lifting up the hands was a silent symbol of one's worship of and dependence upon God (1 Timothy 2:8). Nonverbal communication is a legitimate form, but it is not the most important nor the most articulate way for the believer to communicate.

Personal communication. The best way to communicate to a person is through a person. The best person to use is one who is intimately related to you. That is what God did. He went beyond general revelation to speak more personally and fully to man through the prophets, and then He climaxed His communication and spoke to us in His Son (Hebrews 1:1-3). He continues this incarnational type of communication to the world through Christians—who are intimately related to Him (John 17:18; 20:21). Christ became flesh and "explained" the

Father to the world (John 1:14-18). Now we have this same treasure (truth about God) in our earthen vessels and have the same responsibility to "explain" it to our world (2 Corinthians 4:5-7).

Works and words. How do we go about personally communicating this truth to others? Through two interrelated components—works and words. That is the way Christ did it. He acted and spoke. Performed miracles and taught truth. Did things and said things. People looked at Him. People listened to Him. In the gospel of John there is a consistent emphasis on and interplay between His words and His works.[1] Each communicated authentic, sufficient revelation of itself, and at the same time each supported and reinforced the other.

The believer carries on this same works/words communication pattern. We are *"created in Christ Jesus for good works"* (Ephesians 2:10). We are to be *"rich in good works"* (1 Timothy 6:18). Through the Word we are *"adequate, equipped for every good work"* (2 Timothy 3:17). We are to be both careful and zealous to engage in good *deeds* (Titus 2:14; 3:8). Works don't just exist; they communicate. People see them and glorify God as a result (Matthew 5:16). Wives are to communicate truth to disobedient husbands by allowing them to *"observe your chaste and respectful behavior"* (1 Peter 3:2). Widows are eligible for significant service in the local church on the basis of them having a *"reputation for good works"* (1 Timothy 5:10). People know what kind of person she is by virtue of what she has done. Titus was instructed to *"show yourself to be an example of good deeds"*(Titus 2:7). Peter said, *"Keep your behavior excellent among the Gentiles, so that in the thing in which they slander you as evil doers, they may on account of your good deeds, as they observe them, glorify God in the day of visitation"* (1 Peter 2:12). Paul summarizes the matter well: *"Deeds that are good are quite evident, and those which are otherwise cannot be concealed"* (1 Timothy 5:25).

Works are what we do. The activity of going someplace. Meeting with a group. Calling on a person in the hospital. Taking time to listen. Waiting patiently for someone. Creating the right impression by the way we dress, use makeup, wear jewelry. What we eat and how much. How we spend our money. How we care for our body. Arriving on time. Doing what we said we would do. Cleaning up. Fixing meals. Getting the right amount of sleep. Going to the doctor. Buying what you need. Using your head. Obeying the speed limit. Paying your taxes. Mowing the lawn. Trimming the hedge. Helping the neighbor. Paying the paper boy on time. Fixing the leaky faucet. Carrying out the garbage. Making your bed. Picking up your dirty clothes. Doing the laundry. Taking a vacation. Having new folk over for supper. Not littering. Voting. Not wasting time. Not padding the expense account. Serving on a committee. Paying your dues. Hugging your wife and kids. Remembering anniversaries and birthdays. Doing your homework on time. Studying for the exam. Paying bills promptly. Breaking bad habits. Cultivating good ones.

We could go on and on. Each item involves some kind of personal act. Each act communicates a message.

But life is more than a series of events; more than doing a lot of things. God has given us the capacity to speak as well as act. In most of our actions, words are involved. What we do is normally in the context of what we say. What we say is normally in the context of what we do. The Scriptures recognize this interrelatedness of our words and our works.

James is a good book to study in this regard. The first thing we should note is that words cannot be substituted for works. Note the example in James 2:14-16. If you tell a starving person that you are concerned about his plight and you hope everything will work out okay—and you don't act to meet his need—you have wrongly tried to substitute words for works. Failure to act demonstrates the invalidity of your faith. Words are simply not nutritious enough to meet hunger pangs. A vital, valid faith would give the hungry man something to eat, and that act itself would communicate concern whether it was ever vocalized or not. Words are powerful and can meet many needs, but there are some needs which require more than words.

Now move back in chapter two of James for the case of the usher who caters to the upper class saint while putting down the lower class one. How does he show partiality and favoritism? By what he says to them and where he seats them (v. 3). If he didn't say a word out loud he would still communicate a definite non-verbal message when he personally took the one to a choice front-row padded seat and motioned the other toward a back row bench. But he does speak. Words that pander to one and put down the other.

Step into chapter one for a moment. Verses 26 and 27 say that the religious man will bridle his tongue, visit orphans and widows and remain unstained by the world. Are we to conclude that the epitome of spirituality is to be a mute who makes housecalls and lives a separated life? Hardly. To bridle the tongue is not to clamp it shut but to control it. A ministry to orphans and widows would involve the work of going to see them and the words of instruction and comfort they need. Keeping unstained from the world involves various actions and the appropriate words that go along with the actions, like, "No, I cannot in good conscience take part in that kind of price-fixing scheme." The religious man works with words and through words.

Look at chapter three. Having clearly established the principle that works are the significant evidence of faith (ch. 2), he now proceeds to deal with one aspect of works—the use of words (3:1-12). A teacher works with words. In 3:13-18 the subject is wisdom. It will be evidenced by good behavior and wise deeds performed in gentleness (v. 13). An opposing lifestyle would be bitter jealousy and selfish ambition (vv. 14-15). Where these exist there is disorder and every evil thing (v. 16). How does one demonstrate jealousy? It's hard to get a well-defined "jealous look" on one's face! You do it with words. How does one evidence ambition? Hang an "I am ambitious" sign around his neck? You do it with words. Wisdom, however, is first pure, then peaceable, gentle, reasonable, etc. (v. 17). How does one get a reputation for being peaceable, gentle and reasonable? Not by just acting warm and fuzzy. It takes words. The right words. The chapter closes by saying that you sow seeds that produce righteousness by being a peacemaker (v. 18). You don't make peace by knowing doctrine and smiling and shaking hands. That helps, but the right words are inextricably involved in peacemaking.

Paul integrates works and words too. He tells the Colossians that they used to engage in evil deeds (1:21), but now he is praying that they will get involved in every good work (1:10). In chapter three he lists some of the bad works they are to consider themselves dead to and thus to put out of their current lifestyle. Get rid of *"immorality, impurity, passion, evil desire, and greed"* (3:5). These are things we think about and do. They are works. Yet it would be hard to do any of them without words being spoken. In the same context, believers are exhorted to *"put. . . aside anger, wrath, malice, slander, and abusive speech from your mouth"* and *"not lie to one another"* (3:8, 9). These are certainly word-oriented works.

All of this biblical data is given to alert us to the fact that we communicate as persons to persons, and we accomplish this by what we do (our works) and by what we say (our words). Perhaps an analogy from the world of drama will help. On the stage of life, against the backdrop of general revelation, the Christian has the privilege of communicating through his actions and his speech. Actions alone have all of the potential and all of the limitations of pantomime. The Christian, however, is seldom, if ever, restricted to pantomime alone. He augments and elaborates it with his spoken words. It is his reponsibility to see that his movements and his lines support and reinforce each other and ensure that both are in harmony with the script—the Word of God. To borrow a contemporary cliche—we need to get our act together!

With Whom do we Communicate?

Anyone. Potentially, everyone. Believers are to be in the church and there they are to assemble, encourage, stimulate, teach and admonish one another. Believers are to go into the world and preach the gospel to every creature. We are to share birth truth with the unsaved and growth truth with the saved.

However, if another believer is willfully engaged in sin and refuses to repent, others in the assembly are not to associate with him.[2] The normal pattern of communication is cut off, and that very action in itself transmits a powerful message. Disassociation does not mean total silence, for the ultimate goal of withdrawal is not punishment but restoration. Thus Paul adds to his *"do not associate with him"* the tempering words *"do not regard him as an enemy, but admonish him as a brother"* (2 Thessalonians 3:14,15). Excommunication does not outlaw communication.

We are also to be very careful in our association with false teachers. Paul told Timothy to confront them with their error and to tell them the truth, and at the same time, to avoid their worldly and empty chatter and to refuse to become embroiled in their foolish and ignorant speculations.[3] If the apostate denies the person and work of Christ, John says: don't receive him; don't even greet him (2 John 10, 11).

The Christian is also to be wary of entangling alliances with unbelievers. Our responsibility is to communicate truth to them, but not in the context of an intimate, binding relationship with them (2 Corinthians 6:14-18). The unequal yoke raises our vulnerability to the infection of sin and lowers our vocal-ability to combat it.

Now let's get real personal and practical with this concept. We are to communicate with everyone. Who is it you are not talking to right now? Who are you on the "outs" with? Whom did you vow "never to speak to again"? Do you have any biblical grounds for your attitude and action? Your friend didn't say the right thing; didn't do the right thing. They forgot. They lied. They quit. They left. And you continue to nurse your grudge by inwardly hurling at them. They aren't perfect. They committed an act of sin against you or someone you love. You are going to hold that against them. How long? Until they are perfect? That's too long! Until they come crawling to you on their knees in remorse and repentance? What if they never do? Let the message of the Word massage your bruised, swollen ego:

> *"Let all bitterness and wrath and anger and clamor and slander be put away from you, along with all malice. And be kind to one another, tender-hearted, forgiving each other, just as God in Christ also has forgiven you"* (Ephesians 4:31,32).

> *"Pursue after peace with all men... see to it that no root of bitterness springing up cause trouble...* (Hebrews 12:14,15).

> *"Blessed are the peacemakers, for they shall be called sons of God"* (Matthew 5:9).

> *"If possible, so far as it depends on you, be at peace with all men"* (Romans 12:18).

What a tragedy—when people in the same home, the same community, the same church, the same family, on the same board, in the same business—aren't on speaking terms.

"But wait a minute," you say, "my problem is that so-and-so won't talk to me." "I'm willing, but they're not." What is your responsibility then? It is to faithfully speak the truth in love to them. Whether they listen and respond or not. Keep the channel open from your end. Think reconciliation; not retaliation. Don't take revenge. Don't be pressured into responding in kind. *"Do not be overcome by evil, but overcome evil with good."*[4]

Then there is the problem of communicating with certain selected ones and excluding other ones. If we could label two prime communication problems in the church they would be "cliches" and "cliques." Superficial communicating and selective communication. There were cliques at Corinth. At least four of them. They each rallied around a given leader—Paul, Apollos, Cephas or Christ (1 Corinthians 1:12). Paul urged them to break down these barriers, to stop their jealousy and strife, to quit quarreling, and he classified their attitudes and actions as carnal (1:10-13; 3:3-9).

A similar problem surfaced in Philippi. Two women, Euodia and Syntyche, were hurling at each other. Paul asked these two to "live in harmony" (Philippians 4:2), and instructed the entire congregation to be *"standing firm in one spirit, with one mind striving together for the faith of the gospel"* (1:27). Cliques are built on selfishness and conceit (2:3). They disappear when believers are *"united in spirit"* (2:2). This phrase could be translated literally "souls together." Members of the body of Christ are to be knitted together as soul brothers and soul sisters. Such unity comes when we regard others as more important than ourselves; when we are concerned about their interest as well as our own (2:3,4). The pattern to follow is Christ. He was a member of a clique that was real and legitimate—the Trinity! And He was willing to give up many of the privileges of membership in that group, in order to relate to us and meet our needs. *"Have this attitude in yourselves,"* writes Paul, *"which was also in Christ Jesus"* (2:5-8).

The local church can be a proving ground for love and acceptance. It may also be a spawning ground for distinctions and divisions. People are different. In a given local church you will find differences in age, in race, in sex, in socio-economic levels, in degrees of maturity, in growth rates, in backgrounds, in gifts, in personalities, and in talents. Some of these differences can be changed; some remain fixed.

When people who are different worship, fellowship and serve together, two things can happen. Pride can flourish internally. Cliques can form externally. Along with our differences there must be a deepening commitment to our oneness; a realization that:

"there is neither Jew nor Greek, there is neither slave nor free man, there is neither male nor female; for you are all one in Christ Jesus" (Galatians 3:28).

It won't just happen. It cannot be legislated. All of the members of the body must be *"diligent to preserve the unity of the Spirit in the bond of peace"* (Ephesians 4:3).

How do we Communicate?

We have already explored the answer to this in a more general way. We communicate through our *works* and our *words*. Now let's probe some of the particulars.

Physically. There are many ways to say "I love you." "I am concerned about you." "I want to help you." "I need you." Touching is one of these. In biblical times they exchanged the right hand of fellowship (Galatians 2:9) and said "Hello" and "Goodby" by kissing and embracing (Romans 16:16). Beyond these kinds of expressions, little is said about physical contact in Scripture. Because of sexual implications, Paul said that *"it is good for a man not to touch a woman"* (1 Corinthians 7:1). Good words of advice, because touching can and does have romantic and/or sexual implications between certain people and at certain times. All of us need to exercise discerning caution in this realm. But being cautious should not make us cold and aloof. There are times when acceptance, appreciation, comfort or concern are communicated by talking *and* an appropriate action of physical contact—a hug, an arm around the shoulder, a pat on the back, a squeeze of the hand. Contact communicates. Even people in deep comas often show improved heart rates when their hands are held by someone.

Christ promised the Holy Spirit as another who would come alongside to help (John 14:16). It is difficult to imagine Spirit-filled Christians coming along-side others to help and yet remaining impassively detached. Our daughter brought a college friend home for Easter one year. She had a great time with us and we with her. We took the girls downtown to catch their ride back to school. In my dignified and somewhat inhibited way I said, "We enjoyed having you visit in our home," and reached out to shake her hand. In her spontaneous and uninhibited way she said, "What a fantastic four days. You and your family are wonderful. I love you for letting me be here." And with that she gave me a great big bear hug! Right in the lobby of the Hilton Hotel! A bit embarrassing—to say the least—for a middle-aged man who has been taught (especially as a *man*) not to show too much emotion nor to get too close to people. We can learn some things about communication from the younger generation.

Visibly. We communicate powerfully by our visible attitudes and actions. Truth, incarnated into our lifestyle can be effectively transmitted to others. This is why Paul said to the Corinthians, *"Be imitators of me, just as I also am of Christ"* (1 Corinthians 11:1). In like manner, he told the Philippians to follow his example and others who set the same example (Philippians 3:17; cf. 4:9). He exhorted Timothy to be an example to others (1 Timothy 4:12). In the same passage, Timothy is instructed to so saturate himself with the truth that his *"progress may be evident to all"* (4:15). "Progress" is literally "to cut forward." When one does that he is making progress. It is not a secret progress, however, but a personal growth that is evident to others. To insure that this takes place, Paul tells Timothy to *"pay close attention to yourself and to your teaching"* (4:16). We communicate by example. The home and the church are prime places for this to take place. So parents, parishioners and pastors need to be making the kind of progress that others can see.

Adaptively. All of Paul's letters work on this principle. He adapted his message and his lifestyle to the needs of the recipients. The Corinthians were carnal—evidenced by jealousy and strife. He doesn't mince words with them (1 Corinthians 3:1-3). Later they were unforgiving. He told them to change (2 Corinthians 2:5-11). His evangelistic ministry was based on the principle of adaptation. He never changed the message, but he adapted his methods to fit each given audience (1 Corinthians 9:19-23).

Colossians four gives us added insight on adapting. Paul requested prayer for the ability to *"make it clear in the way I ought to speak"* (4:4). Paul was in prison. His concern was not one of the assembling and audience; the guards changed every eight hours. His concern was his ability to adapt his message to the many different persons and needs with which he came in contact.

He then turns to the ministry of the Colossian Christians and says, *"Let your speech always be with grace, seasoned, as it were, with salt, so that you may know how you should respond to each person"* (4:6). Food is seasoned to make it appetizing and palatable. We are to do the same with our conversation. Especially when interacting with unbelievers. There is no place for routine, dull, insipid evangelism. The word "salt" was often used in similar contexts in extra-biblical Greek to mean "witty." It is possible that that is what Paul has in mind here. Note that it is important how we respond to "each person." We relate and adapt to individuals. Each one is different. This is true in the church also. We are to adapt our communication so that it is given *"according to the need of the moment"* in that other person's life (Ephesians 4:29).

We can be both message-centered and audience-centered without sacrificing quality in either area. So a husband adapts his communication to his pregnant wife. She adapts when he is winding up the fiscal year at the office and has to work late. Parents adapt to the differences in each of their children. Christians adapt to the unique nature and needs of others in the body. Flexibility is our one firm policy.

Patiently. Timothy was a young communicator. His job description was *"to preach the word; be ready in season and out of season; reprove, rebuke, exhort, with great patience and instruction"* (2 Timothy 4:2). Five brisk imperatives tell Timothy what he is to do. Modifying the last three is the phrase *"with great patience and instruction."* Reproving, rebuking and exhorting are ways of applying the truth. One can lose patience with the erring brother who needs reproof. One may omit the reasoned explanation from the fiery, impassioned exhortation. Without patience, we hurl. The recipient becomes an opponent. Without instruction, we hide. We keep to ourselves some things others need to know. The recipient gets heat without light. Warmth does not increase vision. Pleading does not create perception.

People will not always react as soon as we wish they would. As positively as we know they should. We want perfect responders. We will never have them. So, we must develop a fruit of the Spirit—patience. Some individuals don't catch on quickly or easily. They irritate us. They forget what we told them before. This irks us. We want perfect learners. We don't have them. One of the responsibilities this places on us is to continue to develop more and better ways of instructing. We are to be patient, instructive communicators.[5]

1 Thessalonians 5:14 relates patience to three types of individuals. *"And we urge you, brethren, admonish the unruly, encourage the fainthearted, help the weak, be patient with all men."* "Unruly" literally means "without order." It was a military term referring to soldiers out of step or an army in confused retreat. The believer whose life is out of step with God's cadence needs to be admonished. Those doing the admonishing need patience, for you may be working with those who learn slowly and stumble frequently.

The "fainthearted" and "weak" are those who aren't spiritually strong and bold. Those who are easily overwhelmed by the stress and strains of life. They need encouragement and help. But those who are tough, easily get impatient with those who are tender, timid and tense. Patience is needed.

Our words will manifest whether we have it. An edgy "Hurry up." A testy "Oh no, not again." A frustrated "Here, let me do it." A disgruntled "You never seem to get it right." A peeved "Isn't it ready yet?" There are times when we must be honest and confrontive, but we must never lose patience. Only the Spirit of God can enable us to put up indefinitely with imperfect people. We are giving them plenty of opportunities to do likewise.

Peacefully. Others are imperfect, and so are we. Therefore, we will not automatically be at peace with them. Yet it is our God-given responsibility to be peacemakers.[6]

There is no place for cantankerous Christians. No room in the body for the obnoxious, hard-to-get-along-with individual. No spiritual gift equips you to be stubborn, pugnacious, or crabby. No way in the world you can excuse your abrasive personality as simply "the way God made me."

The words of Romans 12:18 are pertinent. *"If possible, so far as it depends on you, be at peace with all men."* The obligation is clear: *"be at peace with all men."* This is inclusive in its scope: *"all men."* Note the reservation: *"if it be possible, so far as it depends on you."* It may not always be possible. But make sure the impossibility is created by your commitment to truth and/or the others person's violation of the same. The believer cannot condone peace at any price. He cannot be at peace with sin and error. There are times when peace must be sacrificed. Yet the overall impact of this verse is that we are to be essentially committed to establishing and maintaining peaceful relations between ourselves and others. And we can, for all it is still quite true that *"when a man's ways are pleasing to the Lord, He makes even his enemies to be at peace with him"* (Proverbs 16:7).

Confidently. What about shy, retiring people who don't say much and when they do, they say it with reticent reserve? They don't think their opinion is worth much. They don't sound too convinced about anything.

A bold authoritative confidence is the picture of the biblical communicator. Not brash or belligerent. Not dogmatic or pontifical. Simply convinced that you are important, that others are important, and that what you have to say is important.

This is especially true of those who minister the Word of God. Paul told Titus to *"speak and exhort and reprove with all authority. Let no one disregard you"* (Titus 2:15). Don't let anyone put you down or pass off what you have to say as unimportant. In the same letter he told him to *"speak confidently"* (3:8). Paul's own words were spoken with *"full conviction"* and *"boldness"* (1 Thessalonians 1:5; 2:2). One may wonder, then, why Paul stated in 1 Corinthians 2:3, 4 that he related to the Corinthians in weakness, fear and trembling, and not in persuasive words of wisdom. Weakness, fear and trembling refer to the apostle's inward sense of his *own* inadequacy. His preaching was not persuasive words of *worldly* wisdom. He was a confident apostle. He was an articulate, persuasive speaker. But his confidence and persuasiveness were demonstrations of the power of the Spirit of God (1 Corinthians 2:4, 5).

It is a temptation to make this a matter of personality rather than spirituality. To simply assert that you are not a dynamic, aggressive person does not justify a wishy-washy, namby-pamby way of communicating. The Spirit of God wants to make you a confident man or woman. He will use your personality, which may mean—in your case—a quiet confidence. He wants to make you a bold partner in the marriage, a forceful parent in the family, a confident communicator in the church and in the world. He will normally do this in the context of your personality, not in contradiction to it. Where your personality causes you to be a weak, insipid purveyor of facts, the Holy Spirit can help you change. Whether teaching a Bible class, greeting a visitor, telling your children a story, or voicing your opinion at the PTA meeting, God expects you to be a confident communicator.

Repetitiously. We tend to forget. The Bible recognizes this and says that one important element of communication is reminding people of what they already know. The Lord told the disciples that He was sending the Holy Spirit to function as the "Divine Reminder" (John 14:26). Peter's words on this subject are basic:

"Therefore, I shall always be ready to remind you of these things, even though you already know them, and have been established in the truth which is present with you. And I consider it right, as long as I am in this earthly dwelling, to stir you up by the way of reminder, knowing that the laying aside of my earthly dwelling is imminent, as also our Lord Jesus Christ has made clear to me. And I will also be diligent that at any time after my departure you may be able to call these things to mind" (2 Peter 2:12-15).

Peter clearly justifies his ministry of reminding. Paul told Timothy and Titus to inculcate reminding into their ministries.[7]

Preachers and teachers often feel uncomfortable reiterating concepts to their people. They shouldn't feel that way. Repetition of truth is biblical. Parents have to do this over and over with their children. That is because children don't always remember. God's children are no different. We need to be reminded.

Consistently. James underlines this point. In chapter three he deals with the problem of the untamed, restlessly evil, poison-laden tongue (v. 8). It causes us to be schizophrenic communicators. We transmit a double message. From the same mouth comes blessing and cursing (vv. 9, 10). *"This ought not to be,"* says James. This is as ridiculous as getting both fresh water and salt water from the same drinking fountain spigot (v. 11). If you are a growing Christian, it will be evidenced by the fact that you are *consistently* speaking words that are wise, pure, peaceable, gentle, reasonable, full of mercy and good fruits, unwavering and without hypocrisy (v. 17). Weigh each word carefully, for the careless word will have to be accounted for.

If we are nice to our customers and grouchy with our employees, something is wrong. If we are friendly in church and sullen at home, something is wrong. If we are profane at the ball game and cultured at the supper table, something is wrong. If we are hostile to our in-laws and hospitable to our own parents, something is wrong. If we are crabby in the morning, until we have had a cup of coffee, something is wrong! We are to be consistently good communicators. Consistency relates to our witness too, for we are to be *"always ready to make a defense to everyone who asks"* us about our faith (1 Peter 3:15).

Cautiously. When you lay out your plans for tomorrow and confidently proclaim: "This is what I am going to do"—be careful. Why? Because you don't know with absolute certainty what will happen tomorrow. Hear what James says:

> *"Come now, you who say, 'Today or tomorrow, we shall go to such and such a city, and spend a year there and engage in business and make a profit.' Yet you do not know what your life will be like tomorrow. You are just a vapor that appears for a little while and then vanishes away"* (James 4:13, 14).

Does this mean we shouldn't plan ahead? Are we to just wander aimlessly into the future? Not at all, for James goes on to say:

> *"Instead, you ought to say, 'If the Lord wills, we shall live and also do this or that'"* (4:15).

We do plan and we do share our plans with others, but we also recognize God as the ultimate planner. There are many things the believer can and should be confident about. But when it comes to the specific details for my life tomorrow, there must always be a submission of all of my purposeful planning to God's sovereign, perfect program. We can be confident when we speak the truth. Cautious when we speak about timetables.

Non-judgmentally. In the final analysis, there is only one Lawgiver and Judge—God. We are warned in Scripture not to assume that role.[8] The reason is our inability to conduct a thorough examination. We look at the outward appearance; God looks at the inner man—the heart (1 Samuel 16:7). He *"will both bring to light the things hidden in the darkness and disclose the motives of men's hearts"* (1 Corinthians 4:5). We cannot do this, therefore we cannot pass final judgment.

Removing ourselves from the judge's seat does not relieve us of the responsibility of being a discerning evaluator of both ourselves and others. We have already spoken about self-evaluation. Later we will deal with our God-given responsibility to evaluate and confront others.

Proudly. Most of the time proud boasting is soundly condemned in Scripture[9] (cf. James 3:5; 4:6; Ephesians 2:9; Proverbs 27:1, 2). But there are some exceptions to this. Note the following:

> *"Therefore, we ourselves speak **proudly** of you among the churches of God for your perseverance and faith in the midst of all your persecution and afflictions which you endure"* (2 Thessalonians 1:4).

> *"For if in anything I have **boasted** to him about you, I was not put to shame; but as we spoke of all things to you in truth, so also our **boasting** before Titus proved to be the truth"* (2 Corinthinas 7:14; cf. 8:24; 9:3, 4).

Paul felt it quite proper to boast about what God was doing in the lives of others. It is right to be proud of God. It is also legitimate to boast about what God has done in our own lives. Paul does this in 2 Corinthians 10-12. These chapters are an interesting study in both the problems and potential of personal boasting. Paul calls specific attention to himself (e.g. 11:18-33; 12:2-5), yet at the same time he comments on how such data can be easily misconstrued, and he is careful to emphasize his weaknesses as well as his strengths (11:30; 12:5). The caption that he puts over all boasting is this: *"He who boasts, let him boast in the Lord"* (10:17). That doesn't rule it out; it just puts rigid restrictions on it.

I commented once on the lovely solo sung by a young woman in worship service. I expressed appreciation for her commitment to the Lord and for her effective use of her talent. I concluded by saying, "We are proud of you, and I know your parents are too." After the service, her parents came to me very upset by my remarks about them being proud of their daughter. "All pride is wrong," they said. "Please don't characterize us as being proud of our daughter." I didn't know enough to press the issue then, but I would now. If Paul spoke proudly about his spiritual children, then we can certainly do likewise about our own children—always recognizing God's prime place in the process.

Discerningly. The maturing believer is developing the capacity to discern between good and evil. This would relate to how we listen as well as to how we speak. The Thessalonians were warned to *"let no one in any way deceive you"* (2 Thessalonians 2:3). There will always be false apostles and deceitful workers whom Satan will use, so we must always be on guard, and with discernment always test the spirits to see whether they are from God.[10] The believer must strain everything through his biblical filter and check it carefully. That includes everything—from what we read in the newspapers and hear and see on television to what we listen to in church, and to what our children tell us.

Graciously. Whatever we say, it ought to be spoken graciously. *"Let your speech always be with grace"* (Colossians 4:6). The word "grace" is quite theological in the Old and New Testaments. It describes God's kindness and favor freely bestowed on us in Christ. When used of our speech it simply means that we employ words that are kind and gracious. When we do this our words will *"give grace to those who hear"* (Ephesians 4:29). This is not saying that the words will always be pleasing to the hearer; but they will be of benefit to them.

Other terms are used to convey the need for gracious words. We are to cull out the *"unwholesome"* word. We are to have speech beyond reproach. We are to be kind and gentle. We are to speak the truth in love.[11] The Lord Jesus was full of grace and truth (John 1:14). His works and His words manifested both. I can think of no two better words to describe the believer's communication—full of grace and truth.

Creatively. The Bible is not a textbook on methodology. But it does give us principles of communication and provides much insight on how to present truth. We have examined some of these principles and methods. Yet the Bible in no way purports to contain all of the ways truth can be presented. The Holy Spirit is the divine communicator resident within us. How many ways does He know and can He use to communicate truth? *An infinite number of ways.* It is our responsibility to be knowledgeable of the biblical principles, sensitive to the given situation, and alert to the leadership of the Holy Spirit. There is no one right way or best way to communicate. There are many, many good ways to speak the truth in love. Certain methods could be inappropriate at certain times, such as discussion when nobody knows anything about the subject. Some methods would be inappropriate at any time, such as brainwashing or other manipulative techniques. Within biblical boundaries we ought to be committed to discovering new ways of transmitting truth.

What do we Communicate?

Truth. This is the umbrella under which everything in this section fits. We are all exhorted to know and speak the truth.[12] But truth can be packaged and presented in various ways and for different purposes. We want to explore some of these different aspects of the truth we are to communicate to each other. You will notice that content and method are interrelated in each of these concepts.

Teaching. The communication of sound doctrine is basic.[13] Concepts about the Bible, God, Christ, the Holy

Spirit, man, sin, salvation, sanctification, Satan, angels, demons, the church and prophecy need to be taught and learned. Teaching is not superficial exposure to these concepts, but an in depth depositing of insight. The Greek word, *didasko,* denotes instruction in its widest sense—the imparting of information, the passing on of knowledge, and acquiring of skills. The understanding of truth, important as it is, is never the final end of teaching. We are to be *"filled with the knowledge of His will in all spiritual wisdom and understanding"*—so that we may *"walk in a manner worthy of the Lord"* (Colossians 1:9, 10). As James puts it, we are to be doers of the Word, not just hearers (1:22). Failure to act on what we know is sin (James 4:17).

Teaching should be a formal, regular, systematic part of the program of the local church. From the pulpit and in the classroom, in large and small groups, truth should be consistently and effectively imparted by gifted members of the body. It is an ongoing process, as indicated by Paul's words to Timothy to entrust truth to faithful men who will *"be able to teach others also"* (2 Timothy 2:2). It is an intergenerational process. Titus was instructed to teach all ages and both sexes and told to motivate the older women to teach the younger women (Titus 2:1-8).

Teaching is also to be carried on informally by all believers in the context of the local church and beyond it. In Colossians 3:16 all of the members of the body are exhorted to teach one another. The home is another basic context for teaching of the truth (Deuteronomy 6:4-9; 2 Timothy 3:14, 15). All Christians should be teaching others and learning from others in both formal and informal settings. One of the best ways to learn truth is to teach it. Regardless of how little you know, there will always be someone you know who knows less. Teach them! Regardless of how much you know, there will always be someone around who knows more and can teach you. Learn from them!

Admonition. Linked inseparably to teaching is admonition. Paul says that he utilizes teaching and admonition to bring individuals to maturity in Christ (Colossians 1:28). He later exhorts every member of the Colossian church to be involved in *"teaching and admonishing one another"* (3:16). The Greek word, *noutheteo,* means to "place in the mind." It denotes the activity of placing corrective concepts in the mind, and carries with it the idea of confronting with a view to correcting. The unruly and disobedient are to be admonished.[14] Paul regularly admonished believers in Ephesus during his three years of ministry there.[15] It was regarded as a normal function of the leaders of the local church, the Old Testament Scriptures, and fathers.[16] Members of the church at Rome were regarded by Paul as *"filled with all knowledge, and able also to admonish one another"* (Romans 15:14).

Confrontation and correction are presented in other ways in Scripture. Note the following:

> *"Those who continue in sin, rebuke in the presence of all, so that the rest also may be fearful of sinning"* (1 Timothy 5:20).

> *"with gentleness correcting those who are in opposition"* (2 Timothy 2:25; cf. 4:2).

> *"... refute those who contradict... reprove them severely that they may be sound in the faith"* (Titus 1:9, 13; cf. 2:15).

> *"Reject a factious man after a first and second warning"* (Titus 3:10).

Out of confrontive, corrective communication can come confession and forgiveness, restoration or where there is no repentence—excommunication.[17]

A lot of teaching and admonition goes on in the natural, normal interaction of believers. When Mary shares with Janet how she is learning to apply biblical principles of discipline more consistently and effectively in rearing her little boy, she may well be *teaching* Janet some things she as a young mother needs to know. If Janet hasn't been consistently putting these principles into operation with her young daughter, she will be *admonished* about her failure to and may resolve to do a better job. All of this biblical teaching and admonishing can take place in a casual conversation over a cup of coffee in the family room.

Body life services where spontaneous and planned sharing takes place are natural contexts for teaching and admonition. When one person relates how she prayed and God answered, others learn about prayer and are admonished in their own prayer habits. When one shares about his witnessing to an unsaved friend, the rest learn about witnessing and are admonished to reach out to their unsaved friends. Could it be that we have so relegated teaching to the classroom and admonition to the closet or courtroom that we are missing the potential of both in the normal interaction of believers? For-

Formal Teaching   Formal Admonition

Informal Teaching & Admonition

mal teaching by gifted men and women is a biblical imperative. It should become the basis for informal teaching by all
of the members of the body. Formal admonition is also a
biblical imperative. If surrounded by the consistent informal
admonition of well-taught believers, formal admonition
would be less needed by the body and less traumatic to the
body when needed and administered. One of the reasons why
church discipline is so difficult to administer is that we
haven't provided the context for it. Suppose a young husband is devoting too much time to his job and too little time
to his wife. But suppose also that he is in a church where a lot
of good formal and informal teaching and admonition is going on. Chances are the church will never have to face the
crisis of disciplining him for running off with his secretary.
Why? Because he is receiving and applying the kind of truth
that he needs. But if discipline does become necessary in his
case the members of that body will be equipped to carry it
out.

Exhortation. We teach doctrine to dispel ignorance. We
provide admonition to deal with disobedience. We add exhortation to cope with apathy and inertia. Doctrine appeals
to the mind. Admonition alerts the conscience. Exhortation
addresses the emotions and the will. Admonition and exhortation are similar, but whereas admonition involves confrontive correction, exhortation emphasizes stimulus and
challenge. Believers need encouragement to do what is right
and to do it well. Exhortation provides just that.

The primary word is *parakeleo* (noun, *paraklesis*), to call
to, to address. It is translated urge, exhort, entreat, encourage. Certain believers are gifted for a significant ministry
of exhortation, but any believer can engage in this activity.[18]

The book of Acts reveals that exhortation and encouragement were basic parts of the follow-up given to new
believers. On his return trip to Lystra, Iconium and Antioch,
Paul invested time *"strengthening the souls of the disciples,
encouraging them to continue in the faith."*[19] The Pauline
epistles serve a similar purpose. Believers are frequently

urged, entreated and exhorted to move toward specific goals, such as: *"present your bodies," "strive together with me in your prayers," "keep your eyes on those who cause dissensions," "no divisions among you," "be imitators of me," "be in subjection," "reaffirm your love," walk in a manner worthy," "live in harmony," "excel still more," "work."*[20] This ministry of exhortation is not just people badgering people to get with it. It is God exhorting us through His servants and His Word.[21]

Two tendencies plague us: complacency and mediocrity. We are satisfied with minimal effort and with minimal excellence. All of us need those words that will serve as a fresh breeze to propel us out of our doldrums. At times we need a hurricane! All of us need words that spur us on to a faster pace, a higher quality. At times we need the whip, too! There is an urgency in Christianity. We are to redeem the time, and we are to redeem it *now.*[22] Lest there be, in any of us, an unbelieving heart, we are to *"encourage one another day after day,"* because *today* is the most important time in our lives (Hebrews 3:12-15).

We are to encourage each other to assemble together regularly and in the assembly we are to encourage one another to live a holy life (Hebrews 10:25-27). In fact, we are to carefully *"consider how to stimulate one another to love and good deeds"* (Hebrews 10:24). The word "stimulate" literally means to incite, to irritate.[23] We are not to be obnoxious naggers, but to carry on an intelligent prodding ministry.

I called my wife one afternoon and told her I was leaving the office and would be home in ten minutes for supper. I hung up and promptly got involved in some (very important?) paperwork and didn't leave the office until nearly an hour later. In the meantime, Audrey put five-year-old Jeanne on her tricycle pulling two-year-old Juli in her red wagon and sent them down to the corner to wait for Daddy. They waited and waited. Daddy didn't come. Finally, they gave up and went home. Later, as Audrey cooly served me my rewarmed supper, she told me what had happened. I was mortified by my failure, and stimulated by her action—to be a more dependable husband and father. The next time I called home before supper, I asked her if she was going to send the kids to the corner. "I may, and then again—I may not," she slyly said. That left me with no choice. I went home—promptly.

A friend told me he was struggling with the temptation to read pornographic literature. He said, "When you meet me during the week, ask me how things are going, and we will both know that you have reference to this area of temptation. Just knowing that you are going to ask about it will stimulate me to resist the temptation."

We need more of this kind of invited, self-imposed exhortation. As God speaks to us about changes we ought to make, we can enlist the help of others to prod us to put them into effect. When we ask others to help us grow, we take a lot of the tension out of admonition and exhortation. In a sense, we give each other the right to nag—biblically. The church and the home are ideal contexts for this to take place.

Comfort. The hesitant need exhortation and encouragement. The hurting need comfort. The same word *(parakaleō)* is used for both concepts. It is translated "comfort" when the context obviously requires it. For example, Paul tells the Corinthians to forgive and comfort a sorrowing brother, lest he be overwhelmed by excessive sorrow (2 Corinthinans 2:7). To those who sorrowed over the death of loved ones, he said, *"comfort one another with these words"* (1 Thessalonians 4:18).

Comfort is not something we generate on our own and pass on to others. Hear what Paul says:

> *"Blessed be the God and Father of our Lord Jesus Christ, the Father of mercies and God of all comfort; who comforts us in all our affliction so that we may be able to comfort those who are in any affliction with the comfort with which we ourselves are comforted by God"* (2 Corinthians 1:3, 4).

Note the interplay between the vertical and the horizontal. God comforts us. We comfort others. The believer is destined to have pressure and problems (John 16:33; Philippians 1:29); there is an ongoing need for comfort. Those who hurt, need help. Those who help best are those who have hurt and have been helped.

Suffering and Rejoicing.

"And if one member suffers, all the members suffer with it; if one member is honored, all the members rejoice with it" (1 Corinthians 12:26).

Providing, of course, communication takes place. Paul's point is that the human body functions like this *naturally.* There is a communication network in each of us that transmits messages consistently and automatically. When the hand hurts, the whole body knows about it. When the headache is gone, the whole body gets the message.

In the church there should be a similar communication network. When one member of a local assembly of believers is struggling with a problem, the rest of the members should be involved in the struggle too. They can and will—*if they know about it.* When one member is successful in an endeavor, the rest of the group should rejoice with him. That will happen—*if they know about it.* The communication system in the body of Christ is to be as open and effective as that of the human body.

Our tendency is to hide; to keep things to ourselves. The two primary things we are prone to keep to ourselves are *failure* and *success.* We feel that Christians aren't supposed to have problems, so when we do, we don't talk about them. We know that Christians aren't supposed to be proud, so when we have success, we tend to keep it to ourselves. The result? We communicate that which is "nice and neutral." It is significant that the Word of God singles out the two areas we tend to remain silent in, and instructs believers to communicate openly and honestly in these areas.

I heard a young college girl share with a group of believers the fact that she had led her roommate to the Lord. The whole body rejoiced with her. Then she told them she thought she was falling in love with an unsaved man and desperately needed to get her emotions in submission to her mind and will. The whole body suffered with her.

As we share truth that instructs, admonishes, exhorts, and comforts, and as we allow people to know what is bothering us and what is exciting us—we will be saying what needs to be said and listening to what needs to be heard. We will be communicating with one another as God desires.

In Summary

In this chapter we have discussed various reasons why we don't communicate well, how we can and should communicate through our works and our words, who should be included in our communication constellation, ways and means of communicating with each other, and insights on the content we are to communicate. All of this should have alerted us to the importance and potential of communicating consistently and effectively with one another.

Interaction

1. Review the educational, historical and sociological factors discussed early in the chapter. How are these factors currently influencing your own interpersonal relationships?

2. Select some of the good deeds from the list on page 169 and discuss in your family or in some other small group what message is being communicated through each activity.

3. "Christians should get along well with everyone." Do you agree?

4. The Salem Alliance Church in Salem, Oregon, takes a few moments in each Sunday morning worship service to allow people to write a note to someone else on "Encouraging One Another" cards which are supplied in the pew racks. The cards are collected and mailed by the church office to the designated people that week. They mail over thirty each week to folk of all ages, both in and beyond their congregation. What other things could a church do to facilitate exhortation and encouragement?

5. "We protect our friends from the truth out of the mistaken notion that it is more important that they *feel* good than that they *be* good." In the light of some of the concepts in this chapter, how would you rewrite this statement? What contribution does Hebrews 12:11 make to this issue?

6. What can we learn about evangelistic communication from Acts 17:1-4?

7. Communication specialists say that a healthy way to relate to others is to make feeling statements, using the first person, e.g. "I am upset." "I feel put down." In the light of the biblical concepts we have studied, is this a valid approach?

8. This chapter is filled with many seed thoughts for further study and discussion. The teacher could assign students (individually or in groups) to do further research on the areas dealt with under *"How Do We Communicate?"* and *"What Do We Communicate?"* The section on *"The Basic Nature of Our Communication with Others"* merits careful presentation and discussion. Role-playing and case studies would be good methods to use to illustrate and apply the various concepts in the chapter. Specific individual and group goals could be set to put some of these biblical principles into effect.

Footnotes

[1]John 4:34; 5:36; 10:25, 32, 33, 38; 14:10-11.
[2]Matthew 18:17; 1 Corinthians 5:9-13; 2 Thessalonians 3:6, 14; Titus 3:10.
[3]1 Timothy 4:1-7; 6:3-5; 2 Timothy 2:14-26.
[4]Romans 12:19-21; 1 Thessalonians 5:15; 1 Peter 3:9.
[5]2 Timothy 2:24; Galatians 5:22.
[6]Matthew 5:9; Romans 14:19; Hebrews 12:14; 1 Thessalonians 5:13; 2 Corinthians 13:11; 2 Timothy 2:24; 1 Corinthians 7:15.
[7]2 Timothy 2:14; Titus 3:1; Jude 5.
[8]James 4:11-12; 1 Corinthians 4:4-5.
[9]James 3:5; 4:6; Ephesians 2:9; Proverbs 27:1-2.
[10]2 Corinthians 11:13-14; 1 John 4:1.
[11]Ephesians 4:29; Titus 2:8; Ephesians 4:32; 1 Thessalonians 2:7; Ephesians 4:15.
[12]Ephesians 4:15, 25; John 8:32; 17:17.
[13]Acts 2:42; Titus 2:1.
[14]1 Thessalonians 5:14; 2 Thessalonians 3:15.
[15]Acts 20:31; cf. 1 Corinthians 4:14.
[16]1 Thessalonians 5:12; 1 Corinthians 10:11; Ephesians 6:4. In each verse the word "instruction" (NASB) is a form of the Greek word noutheteō.
[17]James 5:16; Ephesians 4:32; Galatians 6:1; Matthew 18:17.
[18]Romans 12:8; Hebrews 3:13; 10:25; 1 Thessalonians 5:11.
[19]Acts 14:22; cf. 11:23; 15:31-32.
[20]Romans 12:1; 15:30; 16:17; 1 Corinthians 1:10; 4:16; 16:15-16; 2 Corinthians 2:8; Ephesians 4:1; Philippians 4:2; 1 Thessalonians 4:1, 11; 2 Thessalonians 3:12; cf. 1 Thessalonians 5:14; 1 Timothy 2:1-2; Hebrews 13:19, 22; 1 Peter 2:11; 5:1-3.
[21]Acts 11:23-24; Romans 15:4-5; 2 Corinthians 5:20; 6:1; 1 Thessalonians 2:2, 3, 11.
[22]Ephesians 5:15-17; Galatians 6:10; Colossians 4:5; 2 Corinthians 6:1-2; Romans 13:8-14; Matthew 5:6.
[23]The word is also used in Acts 15:39 and 1 Corinthians 13:5.

Resources

1. For insight on the various biblical words referred to in this chapter consult *Theological Dictionary of the New Testament,* edited by G. Kittel and G. Friedrich, 10 volumes, published by Eerdmans.

2. For insight on our fragmented, isolated society see *A Nation of Strangers* by Vance Packard, David McKay Co., 1972.

3. For insight on interpersonal relationships in the church: *Caring Enough To Confront* by David Augsburger, Regal Publications; *Building Up One Another* by Gene Getz, Victor Books; *God's Forgetful Pilgrims* by Michael Griffiths, Eerdmans; *Crowded Pews and Lonely People* by Marion Jacobsen, Tyndale; *Building People through a Caring Sharing Fellowship* by Donald Bubna, Tyndale.

4. For insight on integrating psychology and theology: read the quarterly *Journal of Psychology and Theology,* published by Rosemead Graduate School of Psychology, 1409 North Walnut Grove Ave., Rosemead, CA 91770.

Chapter 10

The Results of Good Communication

*I*s God's ultimate purpose to produce skilled listeners and fluent talkers? Not really. Communication is the means to an end. The end is twofold—maturity and unity.

WE GROW UP.........THAT'S MATURITY

WE GROW TOGETHER.....THAT'S UNITY

What makes these two results occur? The effective communication of truth. The truth we depend on to produce growth *in us* functions as the bonding agent to effect unity *between us*. The diagram on the following page visualizes this. Sharing the truth with each other causes us to move toward Christlikeness and toward each other.

For example, if I am struggling with a problem at work, I need to feel free to talk it over with my wife. My tendency is to keep such things to myself. I am still very much afflicted with the "strong-men-can-do-it-by-themselves" syndrome. But when I open up and share it with Audrey, it helps me grow. It is a step of maturation for me in a number of ways. I admit a personal need. That is a step of growth. I verbalize it to someone else. A step of growth. I gain personal insight by

We Grow in Maturity and Unity as we share Truth between Us

listening to my review of the problem. More growth. Audrey may respond with helpful insights. Growth continues. We may decide on a solution, or decide that right now there is no solution. I will just have to tough it out. More growth. Obviously not just for me. In the context of the discussion, Audrey will grow, too.

But letting her in on my inner thoughts and feelings does something else. *It draws us closer together.* Allowing her to ask questions, make suggestions and even to suffer together with me, deepens the intimacy of our relationship. The act of communication has tremendous potential. When the truth is shared, the participants can grow up and together. That which edifies—unifies.

Christ underscored these two objectives in John 17. He prayed that believers would be sanctified and unified (vv. 17-23). Paul told the Ephesians the same thing—preserve unity and attain maturity (4:3, 13). The Colossians got the same message. Strip off the old and put on the new. That's growth. And put on love, the perfect bond of unity. That's togetherness (3:8-14).

Words and Maturity

The progress of other believers is tied directly to what we say to them. Paul told believers to speak the truth in love and that would cause people to grow. He went on to say that there are some words that are unproductive. Delete those and utilize only those words which will build up others.[1] He classified all of his authoritative words to the Corinthians as especially designed to build them up.[2] Words provide the data we need to accurately and adequately program ourselves and others for personal growth.[3]

The church is a natural setting for this to take place. So is the home.

We who are parents tell our children what they need to know. This helps them grow. Our children also communicate things to us that help us grow. For example, their disobedience constitutes an opportunity for our growth. It reinforces our understanding of the truth that *"all have sinned and fall short of the glory of God"* (Romans 3:23). Even our own children! It forces us to establish rules for our kids and to enforce them with fair and consistent parental authority. The child's inconsistent, immature behavior creates a need for him to observe a consistent, obedient set of parents. As a result of all of this, we grow. So the child's "I don't wanna" or "she hit me first" are words that can do more than inform and irritate us. They can also edify us.

Words and Unity

The members of the Trinity have unity to the degree of infinity. They want Christians to experience a similar unity at the level of the finite. The right words facilitate this unity. Paul exhorts the believers in Ephesus to maintain unity. How? By being humble, gentle, patient and forbearing.

These qualities are manifested by the words one chooses to use.

Colossians 3:14-16 talks about ministering to one another in a setting of peaceful unity. How is it attained? Verses 8-11 indicate what you *don't say* to create and maintain unity. Verses 12-13 point out what you *do say* to achieve oneness. Simple avoidance of saying the wrong things does not in itself create unity. We must also say the right things.

Romans 14 deals with the same issue. Each person is to be fully convinced in his own mind about what is right and what is wrong (v. 5). That is a mark of maturity. But maturity not only has personal convictions, it also has interpersonal concern. If I cause a weaker brother to stumble, I may disrupt our unity. Thus I am to say and do that which produces peace between us as well as edification in us (v. 19).

A classic New Testament example of the relationship between the communication of truth and unity is in the Corinthian church. The assembly was riddled with jealousy and strife. The reason? Failure to assimilate solid spiritual food (1 Corinthians 3:1-3).

Love is the melody line that runs through the symphony of unity. Love is sharing with others what you have that they need. When they need a kind word, love provides it. Unkind remarks drive people away. Kind words draw people up close.

We have shown from Scripture that the communication of truth is vital for personal maturity and interpersonal unity. Now we need to explore certain aspects of these two concepts.

The Nature of Truth

When we refer to "truth" as the ingredient necessary to create and maintain unity and maturity, what are we talking about? First and foremost: biblical principles and precepts. *"Thy word,"* said Christ to the Father, *"is truth"* (John 17:17). So if I say to my wife, "God loves you," I am communicating a basic, biblical precept to her. Those words can contribute to our maturity and our unity.

What if I say, "I love you?" I am communicating in harmony with biblical principles, for I am to love my wife (Ephesians 5:25). One way to do this is to tell her I love her. These words can edify and unify us. If I say it and don't mean it, I am violating a biblical principle, for my love is to *"be without hypocrisy"* (Romans 12:9). If well-disguised, my words may edify and unify for the moment, but eventually my subterfuge will be discovered (Numbers 32:23; Galatians 6:7, 8).

What if somone asks me how I am and I say "Fine," but actually I feel depressed about a mistake I just made? The Bible says we are not to lie to one another. Am I guilty of lying? It depends on the persons involved and the timing. We are to bear one another's burdens. Is this a person who can bear it? Is this the right time to unload it? If so, it would be wrong not to share it. We are also to teach one another. Am I applying truth to my own situation? Could this person profit from my experience? Is it the appropriate time for me to share? If the answer is affirmative to all these questions, then it would be right to be honest and communicate with insight. We are also to bear our own load (Galatians 6:5). Am I learning how to do this? Or do I tend to lean on others too much? Can this person really give me biblical counsel? Perhaps this is one of those times I need to work it through internally. The members of the body are to encourage and build up one another. Is this a mature, solid saint who could do that for me? Is now the best time? Then I should open up and allow another member of the body to function. This is one of the benefits of being in the body of Christ. You can share and others will care.

So "Fine" could be right in some instances and wrong in others. To be honest does not mean we tell everybody everything all the time. It means we say what needs to be said to the right person at the right time. Dishonesty is not simply hiding what you know. It is failing to say what ought to be said. Some share too much with too many too often. They need to develop the capacity to carry more of their own load. Others share too little with too few too infrequently. They need to let others help them carry their burden.

Is there truth outside the Word of God? If a wife tells her husband that she is irritated by his frequent failure to notify her when he will be late for supper, is that truth? Certainly it is. It is an honest expression of her true feelings. Sharing them can help both of them grow up and grow together. If a teenager fires a salvo of rebellious words at his parents, though the words may be wrong in terms of their content and intent, still they represent the true reality of what he is thinking and feeling at the moment. The parents must seek to listen and respond with truth that is biblically oriented.

If the doctor tells me to work and eat less, sleep and exercise more, do I have the right to put his words aside because they don't have a chapter and verse with them? Absolutely not. At that point the medical profession is giving me a word of truth designed to edify me according to my physical need of the moment.

The point is that when we speak to each other we don't normally quote Scripture nor validate our concepts with biblical references. We just say what we think. Tell how we feel. Call it like we see it. Share our fears and frustrations. Our ideas and goals. What we say, then, is *always true* in the sense that it is a statement of what is *real* to us. It may not be true in the sense that it is *right,* however. We ultimately determine whether reality is right or wrong by submitting it to the Word of God. If it is in harmony with the Word or does not violate the Word, it is rightly true or truly right.

The wife in our example is angry and admonishes her husband because of his failure to act lovingly to meet her needs, to call her when he will be late. Her anger and admonition are biblically legitimate. They are not only real, they are right. His apology would be the same. Her forgiveness should follow suit.

The rebellious teenager expressed that which is real, but in the light of Ephesians 6:1, 2, that which is wrong. The doctor didn't tell me to do anything in opposition to the Word. The facts that he did give me came from the world of science and medicine. God made that world too, and so, to the extent that man has rightly interpreted the data, he has discovered other areas of truth. When my wife tells me to slow down, her message may be far less medically oriented, but just as true.

All of the truth that brings unity and maturity ultimately comes from God. Much of it comes directly from the Scriptures. They are our primary and inerrant source of truth. Some of it comes through the natural world and the people in it. We must listen carefully to both sources and we must speak carefully from both sources. We must always check to make sure that the truth of the world is in harmony with the truth of the Word. Truth is not limited to the Scriptures, but it is limited by the Scriptures.

The Problem of Hypocrisy

The Greek word *hypokrinomai* means to interpret. It was used of an actor, for that is what he did. He interpreted the poet or playwrite to the general populace. Sometimes he wore a mask to do this, to show that he was not portraying himself but another person—represented by the mask. Slowly, the word was applied to people in real life who were acting—people who wore masks and pretended to be something different from what they really were. Hypocrites they are called. Hyprocrisy is what they engage in. Hiding is another term for it.

Because we all have this capacity for hypocrisy, we can fake both maturity and unity. The infant in us, under the pressure of pride, can be made to act like a grownup. The disunity among us, under the same presure, can be made to appear as harmony.

Satan is a great deceiver—the master hypocrite (Revelation 12:9). He can *"disguise himself as an angel of light"* (2 Corinthians 11:14). He worked his wiles on Eve. She did the same things to Adam (1 Timothy 2:14; Genesis 3:1-6). It has been going on ever since. The scribes and Pharisees did it (Matthew 23:1-39). Judas did it (John 12:4-6; 13:18-30). Peter did it (Galatians 2:11-14). Ananias and Sapphira did it, and paid a terrible price (Acts 5:1-11).

Deceitful hypocrisy moves in many areas. It can be used to disguise the true nature of our giving, our praying and our fasting (Matthew 6:1-18). We can pretend in the key areas of faith and love (Romans 12:9; 2 Corinthians 6:6; 1 Timothy 1:5; 2 Timothy 1:5). For some people, hypocrisy is difficult. Their sins are too conspicuous to hide. Others hide them so well that it takes time to uncover their misdeeds (1 Timothy 5:24). On the other hand, it is hard to hide one's good qualities very long (1 Timothy 5:25). Righteousness filters through the facade.

From this brief survey of what the Word says about hypocrisy and deceit, we can see that we can give others a variety of false messages about ourselves—who we are, what we know, what we have done and can do, what we believe and how we feel. Hypocrisy and deceit also involve the communication of false doctrine. The Bible points this out and soundly condemns it. It condemns, for example, false teaching on the deity of Christ (1 John 4:1-3), on the second coming of Christ (2 Thessalonians 2:3), on the importance of the believer's life-style (Ephesians 5:3-6; 1 Corinthians 6:9), or on anything contrary to the teaching of Scripture (Romans 16:17, 18). Hyprocrites mask truth about themselves and about God.

So it is possible for us to have a semblance of maturity. We say the right things. We engage in the right acts. We go to the right meetings. In the process we mask our fears and failures. Our ignorance and inadequacies. We say "Yes, I know that," when we don't. "Sure, I can do that," when we can't. "I have no problems in that area," when we do. If God uses us to help others to be saved and to grow by our hypocritical words and deeds, it is in spite of us, not because of us. Paul spoke to this issue in Philippians 1:15-18. Some were preaching Christ with the right motive. Some with the wrong motive. Paul rejoiced that Christ was preached regardless of the motive behind it. That did not mean Paul rejoiced in their deceitful, hypocritical attitudes. He was solidly committed to the principle that the will of God was to be done from the heart in every area of life (Ephesians 6:6).

It is also possible for us to make believe we are all one in the Spirit, when we are not. We can act like we are friendly and in agreement, when in fact we are hiding some things that need to be shared. Behind this tranquil scene some clandestine clobbering of one another may also be going on. Believers can be surreptitiously stabbing one another, while giving the outward appearance of unity and harmony. We vote for it, but we have unexpressed reservations. We are involved in the same project, but we aren't on the same team. We serve together, but we think apart. We act friendly, but we feel hostile. We are masters at masking our mediocrity and our mutiny.

It takes wisdom to effect maturity. It takes love to produce unity. The Bible says that the wisdom that is from above is without hypocrisy (James 3:17), and love, too, is to be without hypocrisy (Romans 12:9). The deceiving aspect of all of this is that hypocrisy can initially allow us to achieve the same results that genuineness would give. The counterfeit can appear quite authentic. Eventually and inevitably, however, the pretense will begin to peel away, exposing both the shallow superficiality of the facade and the deceitfulness of the heart (Galatians 6:7, 8). When we talk about unity and maturity, we are talking about the *real* thing.

The Problem of Poor Reception

When I tell my child the truth she needs to know, will it always promote growth in her life and unity between us? When the pastor preaches the Word will it immediately edify and unify those who hear? When a husband tells his wife she is too lenient with the children, will she automatically accept the message and change, and will they draw closer together as a result of his words of needed truth? Ideally, the answer to all of the above situations is "Yes." Realistically, the answer is "not always."

Why not? It isn't the fault of the truth. It is powerfully able to accomplish God's desire (Isaiah 55:11; Hebrews 4:12, 13). Nor is it the fault of the Holy Spirit. He is tied directly to the Word and cannot fail to function (Ephesians 6:17; John 14:26; 15:26; 16:13, 14). If we don't get the results of more growth and greater unity in every truth communication situation it isn't God's fault; it is ours. Because we are imperfect and immature senders and receivers we can talk and listen and neither grow up nor grow together. The problem may reside in the one giving the communication. We have talked about this and mentioned ways of doing a better job of sharing the message (chapter 9). The problem may also reside in the one receiving the communication. Let's think about that for a moment.

Let's look at an unbeliever, as an example. He doesn't always get the gospel message because it is foolishness that he can't understand (1 Corinthians 2:14). Satan contributes significantly to the mental blindness of the natural man (2 Corinthians 4:4; cf. Ephesians 4:17, 18). Only the Holy Spirit can open these closed minds (John 16:7-11).

The believer may also be *"dull of hearing"* (Hebrews 5:11). After *"explaining everything privately"* to His disciples, Christ took them out on a stormy lake and tested their comprehension and appropriation of the truth. They flunked (Mark 4:33-41). After watching Him feed thousands from a lad's lunchbasket, they still worried about where their next meal was coming from. "Haven't you gotten the message yet?" He asked (Mark 8:14-21). He posed a similar question to Phillip: *"Have I been so long with you, and yet you have not come to know Me?"* (John 14:9). He was the Master Teacher, but they *still* didn't get the message. They missed numerous opportunities to grow. They fell miles short of unity (Luke 22:24; Matthew 20:24).

Why this slowness in assimilating truth? First, it is truth from and about God. His thoughts are infinitely higher than ours (Isaiah 55:8, 9), and as such, are not grasped easily and naturally. The divine text requires a divine teacher—the Holy Spirit. Second, our minds aren't all they could or should be. The world, the flesh and the devil have added to the corruption already present in man's self-centered, sin-scarred mind (Romans 1:28; 8:5-8; Ephesians 2:1-3; 4:17, 18; Colossians 1:21). Receiving and assimilating truth is not an automatic process for the Christian. The mind needs renewing (Romans 12:2; Ephesians 4:23; Colossians 3:10), refocusing on things above (Colossians 3:2), and every thought has to be taken captive and put in submission to Christ (2 Corinthians 10:5). We not only receive poorly, we also forget easily. Paul often reminded his readers that what he was writing was something they had been exposed to before and should know. He chides them for not remembering and applying the truth (1 Corinthians 6:15-20; 9:13, 24).

Even though we are Christians, we aren't inherently good listeners and learners—especially when it comes to grasping God's Word. It is quite understandable that Paul often prayed for believers to gain more knowledge, understanding, wisdom and enlightenment (Ephesians 1:17, 18, 19; Colossians 1:9, 10). So that's one reason why truth doesn't always edify and unify. People don't understand it. We must cooperate with the Holy Spirit in both the transmitting and receiving process, if real understanding is to take place.

The Problem of Personal Rejection

There is another reason why shared truth is not always and immediately effective. The preceding reason dealt with the nature of the receiver. This deals with the nature of the truth. Truth not only informs; it convicts. It reproves. It corrects. It zeros in on our sinfulness. We are not always open and receptive to being called on the carpet. We may react negatively. We do this by—

Rejecting the Truth...
>which hinders our personal maturity

and by

Rejecting the Person who gave us the truth...
>which hinders our interpersonal unity.

Rejecting the Truth

The picture above describes what we are saying. We don't like what the person says to us. It is the kind of truth that hurts. Our reaction may be to go on the defensive and refuse to accept either the insight or the individual. But when we reject needed truth, we don't grow up. When we reject the people who share it, we don't grow together.

Paul had this kind of experience with the Christians in Corinth. He writes to confront them with the truth they needed to hear. He doesn't mince words. He says they are quarreling (1 Corinthians 1:11), they are fleshly (3:3), they are arrogant (4:6,18), they haven't reacted properly to sexual sin (5:2), they haven't followed his instructions and disciplined a certain person (5:9-13). He says their inability to handle disputes in the assembly is shameful (6:5). He accuses them of wronging and defrauding one another (6:8). He says he can't praise them because the bad outweighs the good in their lives (11:17). He brings his second letter to a close by giving them advance warning that when he visits them again he will not spare any sinner who needs confrontation (2 Corinthians 13:2). He is firmly committed to the communication of truth (13:8), not just to inform, but to test their obedience (2:9).

The question is: How did they react to these words of confrontive, corrective truth? With open arms? Hardly. Being fleshly, immature babes, their reception was poor. Their feelings were hurt by some of his words and they were unable to immediately respond in a mature way (1 Corinthians 2:14-3:4). They felt like he was tearing them down and for awhile completely missed the point that his severe, authoritative words of truth were to build them up (2 Corinthians 13:10). As a result, the relationship between them was strained, at best. *"My heart is wide open toward you,"* said Paul, *"But you are restrained in your affections toward me"* (2 Corinthians 6:11, 12).

The key word he uses to describe their reaction is *"sorrow"* (2 Corinthians 2:1-4; 7:8). No doubt it was the kind of sorrow that mixes sadness and madness. Babies respond with a cry of "militant unhappiness" when told they must stop doing one thing and start doing another. Spiritual babes react the same way. We get moody and pout. Our pouting may get hostile. When we get hostile, we hurl. Our reaction goes something like this:

> "You told me I was wrong...that made me feel bad...I don't like to feel bad...you are the one who made me feel bad...so...I don't like you... besides...who are you to tell me I was wrong!"

That is the way children relate to their parents. Employees to their employers. The pastor to his board. Students to teachers. Wives to husbands. And in each case, vice versa. Undoubtedly, the Corinthians experienced a similar reaction. During that time they weren't growing, nor were they relating well to Paul or to each other.

When they finally did obey, however, disciplining the immoral individual in their midst, some of them went to the other extreme and wanted to overdo the whole thing. They wanted to continue his excommunication even after his repentance. Paul had to urge them to forgive him, love and accept him (2 Corinthians 2:7-9). Sometimes we, too, over-react. Reprimanded for being impolite, we then go out of our way to be sickeningly sweet! If our ego has been badly damaged by the behavior of one of our children, we may impose punishment that is far too severe.

Eventually, the Corinthians got themselves squared away. Their rejection of the truth and Paul was not a permanent one. Listen to Paul's words:

> *"...I see that that letter caused you sorrow, though only for a while—I now rejoice, not that you were made sorrowful, but that you were made sorrowful to the point of repentance; for you were made sorrowful according to the will of God..."*
> (2 Corinthians 7:8, 9).

The kind of unhappiness that God wants is unhappiness with our sin. A *"godly sorrow"* Paul calls it, that will produce a *"repentance without regret"* (2 Corinthians 7:10, 11). Until that takes place, we remain in disobedience and disharmony. When it happens, we begin to grow toward Christlikeness and toward each other (cf. 2 Corinthians 7:11-16).

What we have been saying is this: The truth is designed to make us to *be* like Christ and to *like* each other. But when we resist and rebel against it, both of these purposes will be thwarted, until we choose to obey. Ideally, we should respond with immediate obedience. When we don't, the result can be prolonged periods out of fellowship with the Lord and out of fellowship with each other. Truth is designed to build us and to bond us. Building and bonding are not always immediate nor are they automatic. Both require our personal, obedient response.

The Problem of Imperfection

How much do we put up with in order to achieve and maintain unity? Remember, we are imperfect people seeking to develop unity and maturity. As a result, there will *always* need to be forbearance and a love that covers a multitude of sins (Ephesians 4:2; Colossians 3:13, 14; 1 Peter 4:8). Imperfect people cannot achieve perfect maturity and unity. Both are dynamic and progressive. Unity is something we must diligently work to maintain (Ephesians 4:3). Maturity is something we have to reach forward to and press on toward (Philippians 3:13, 14).

Realistically, there will always be personal attitudes and actions militating against unity. For example, Paul and Barnabas got into a heated argument over whether Mark would go on a journey with them (Acts 15:37-40). We are not told if one was right and the other wrong. We are simply told that they strongly disagreed and separated. If there was bitterness and an unforgiving spirit on the part of either one, that would have been wrong. As to the reasons for and the legitimacy of the argument and the separation, we are left in the dark. Maybe both of them were right. Paul arguing for the importance of the ministry; Barnabas for the importance of the man. Or, maybe both of them were wrong. One thing for sure: neither of them was perfect.

To put up with imperfection in order to have unity is not to say that we sacrifice holiness for harmony. The principle in 2 Corinthians 6:14-17:1 is that holiness takes precedence over all human relationships (cf. 1 Corinthians 5:9-13). The believer must develop the kind of sensitive maturity that knows whether the situation demands toughness or tolerance. Many of us find it difficult to attain the proper balance. Our perfectionist tendencies make us too tough and our desire to get along with everyone all the time makes us too tolerant. The solution is not to find some middle of the road position and stick to it at all times, but to be able to assess a given situation with biblically based discernment and determine whether it calls for toughness or tolerance. A study of Christ's relationships with different people in different situations will provide rich insight on when and how to be flexible; when and how to be firm. He was both; and He was perfect.

The Development of Unity

It doesn't just happen. We must work at unity. How does this take place? We have already said that it happens as we share truth with each other. That places the emphasis on the truth, and rightly so. Let us also focus on the persons doing the communicating. That is what Paul does in Philippians 2:2. He says: *"make my joy complete—*

"by being of the same mind"	—intellectual unity
"maintaining the same love"	—social unity
"united in spirit"	—emotional unity
"intent on one purpose"	—volitional unity

Paul is deeply conscious of the different dimensions of the human personality, and thus, the different facets of human relationships. The designations that I have given to these four areas are not the only ones that could be used, but they should be helpful in analyzing how we relate to people. Let's add three more dimensions to this relational profile to give it completeness.

Relating to each other through —physical unity
the use of the various senses,
e.g. seeing, hearing, touching

Relating properly in the sexual —sexual unity
realm, to those of the same sex
and to those of the opposite
sex.

Relating to each other in terms—spiritual unity
of growth and ministry, e.g.
praying, studying,
worshipping, serving.

Though the passage in Philippians does not specifically
refer to these three areas, other portions of the Word of God
do. Physical relationships have been discussed earlier in this
book. It involves such things as the right hand of fellowship,
eating together, assembling together, etc., all of which create
the potential for contact and communication, verbal and
nonverbal. Sexual intercourse is designed for the marriage
relationship and is a powerful and profound aspect of the
unity between a husband and wife (Genesis 2:24; 1 Corinthians 7:2-5). In the broader sense, our sexuality plays a part
in all of our relationships, with those of the same sex and
those of the opposite sex. It is beyond the scope of this book
to treat this area, but it is an important one and needs more
biblical and practical attention. All communication in some
way involves our sexuality and all relationships in some way
involve our sexual roles and responsibilities.

Spiritual unity is the most obvious and the most frequently referred to in Scripture. In a sense, it encompasses all
the other areas of unity and draws them together in the individual person, just as it draws persons together in Christ.
The words of Galatians 3:28 beautifully call attention to our
spiritual union with Christ and our unity with each other:

*"There is neither Jew nor Greek, there is neither
slave nor free man, there is neither male nor
female; for you are all one in Christ Jesus."*

We are whole persons, and therefore as we develop unity
with one another we do so with all of the elements of our personhood and personality. For example, we are intellectual beings. We have the capacity to think. We develop unity in this
area by *learning to think together.* Note well, *I did not
say—learning to think alike.* It may involve learning to think

alike, but it doesn't have to and it won't always. We are different, distinct, unique individuals. We are imperfect and immature. We won't always think alike. But we are biblically bound to develop unity, so we must learn to think together. You can't hide and do this. You can't hurl and do this. You must share openly, honestly and appropriately your thoughts and allow the other person(s) to do the same. Effective, consistent dialogue is the key.

Husbands and wives don't always think alike. They discover this the moment they start rearranging the living room furniture. The moment they decide to hang pictures on the wall! But a marriage is to develop unity. Husbands and wives must learn to think together.

Pastor and people don't always think alike. They discover this when the order of service is changed, when plans are being drawn up for the new auditorium, when the pastor's job description is being written. But the church is to have unity. Clergy and laity must develop the skills of thinking together.

Do you sense what we are doing? We have taken one of the seven areas of unity and developed it at the practical level. That is where unity is developed and maintained. It happens in the home, the church, the neighborhood, the office, the shop, the car, in the committee, in the board meeting, in the class, in the dorm, in the study group, on the date, over the phone or in a letter. Each of the seven areas of unity can be explored in the same way. We list them with a few suggestions in each case.

We develop INTELLECTUAL UNITY...
by learning to THINK TOGETHER

Doing such things as discussing, asking, answering, probing, pondering, revealing, clarifying, explaining, restating, etc. Seeking to understand rather than undermine. Working toward a meeting of meaning, not just a meeting of minds. Not always alike, but together.

We develop SOCIAL UNITY...
by learning to FELLOWSHIP TOGETHER

Doing such things as visiting, playing, eating, traveling, picnicking, recreating, walking, jogging, vacationing, hobbying, loafing, talking, attending, relaxing, and the myriad of other things we do as social beings. Together, yes. Alike, not always.

We develop EMOTIONAL UNITY...
by learning to FEEL TOGETHER

Emotions play a vital role in our relationships. We don't always experience and express the same ones, nor in the same way, but we have to learn to accept and appreciate these different feelings if we are to grow together emotionally. Even mature people will not always feel alike.

We develop VOLITIONAL UNITY...
by learning to DECIDE TOGETHER

Decision-making is crucial for unity. We won't always want to do it, or do it the same way. But things must get done, so decisons must be made. Deciding together means we commit ourselves totally, not partially, to the decision. Both (or all) are willing to live with the consequences. No room for "I told you it wouldn't work," "I was never for it anyway." To decide together, when you don't think alike, requires (and produces) maturity.

We develop PHYSICAL UNITY...
by learning to BE TOGETHER

We smile, frown, wink, shrug, gesture, wave, beckon, run, sit, stomp, stand, kick, slouch, touch, push, hug, hold, kiss. With our multi-faceted body language, we relate—using all of our senses. Tone of voice, facial features, posture of body, etc. convey attitudes of acceptance, apathy and alienation. Closeness, yes. Sameness, no.

We develp SEXUAL UNITY...
by learning to LIVE & LOVE TOGETHER

Husbands and wives relate uniquely in the sexual realm. Realizing they are not alike in sexual drives, needs and interest, they must work at learning to make love together. Singles must learn to relate sexually to themselves, to other singles, and to those who are married. All of us must learn to relate to those of the same and opposite sex—especially in the church where male/female roles and responsibilities are spelled out in Scripture. In a rich variety of ways, men and women are not alike, yet they must learn to live and love together.

We develop SPIRITUAL UNITY...
by learning to SERVE & GROW TOGETHER

We meet, pray, study, teach, preach, learn, share, minister, witness, counsel, worship, confess, commit, believe, obey—and all the other things believers do in the church, the home and the world as we live out our biblical responsibilities. Yet because of background, training, age, sex, experience, personality, spiritual gifts, spiritual commitment—we don't all grow at the same rate, we don't all serve in the same way, we don't always worship alike, we don't all occupy the same positions. For both good and bad reasons, there is a tremendous diversity in the body. In the context of all of these differences, we are to learn to worship, serve and grow together.

Interaction

1. What things are hard for you to discuss, even with people you are close to?

2. The issue of whether we should tell everybody everything all the time merits further discussion. Do you agree with the approach taken in this chapter? Why? Why not?

3. Discuss the following:
   * The times when my parents told me some things that really helped me grow up.
   * The times when I rejected my parents and what they told me.
   * The times in our marriage when sharing personal thoughts and feelings brought us closer together.

4. What are some of the typical things we do to give others the impression we are mature? Unified?

5. What are some of the pressures that cause us to be hypocrites?

6. What kinds of truth do you willingly and easily accept from others? What kinds of truth do you resist and reject?

7. Do you tend to be tough or tolerant? In what situations?

8. Explore how you, in your relationships with significant others, have had to learn to develop unity in each of the seven different areas. For example, how do you and your marriage partner differ emotionally. How have you and your children dif-

fered volitionally? What effect have intellectual differences had on the unity of the board or committee or staff you serve on? What are some of the problems a single person has relating to married people in the church?

9. In teaching the material in this chapter make sure the basic concepts of growing up and growing together are communicated with plenty of practical application. Help people explore what kind of truth causes them to grow up, what kind of truth causes them to grow together, and when do the opposite results occur. Stimulate them to set personal, specific goals in the areas of unity and maturity.

Footnotes

[1] Ephesians 4:14, 29
[2] 2 Corinthians 10:8; 13:10
[3] Acts 20:32; 2 Thessalonians 2:15; 1 Timothy 4:6

Resources

For insights on communication for unity and maturity the following are recommended:
A Theology of Christian Education by Lawrence O. Richards, Zondervan, 1975.
How To Be A People Helper by Gary Collins, Vision House, 1976.
The Secret of Staying in Love by John Powell, Argus Communications, 1974.
Body Life by Ray C. Stedman, Regal Books, 1972.

Conclusion

*T*ransparency is traumatic. Open communication is like getting an immunization shot. It hurts, but it helps. If you are looking for painless ways to grow toward each other and toward maturity, call off the search. In God's sovereign plan, a certain amount of discomfort is built into the growing process.

Where do you need to grow up? Open yourself up to the truth in these areas. Let the Word of God invade you. Where do significant others in your life need to grow? Be willing to say what needs to be said to stimulate their growth. Invading lives with truth is risky business. But you are not on your own. God is in that business.

With whom do you need to grow closer together? Work on speaking the words which remove walls and build bridges. Words like this won't always come easy. It is hard to admit failure. It may not be easy to express feelings. It is traumatic to take down the no trespassing sign and invite others to step in. But at the same time, it is so fulfilling to accept and be accepted, love and be loved.

Your relationship with God can be a working model for all other relationships. He is the Master Communicator.

Listen to Him. He will always tell you what you need to know. Talk to Him. He will always listen to anything you have to say. This kind of dialogue with God will equip you to engage in healthy, holy communication with yourself and others. The kind of communication where you will listen carefully to what others have to say. Where you will speak truthfully what others need to hear. When you do this, you and others will grow up—and grow together.

A word to the wise, they say, is sufficient. All of the words in this book have been addressed to you, the wise ones. I trust they will be sufficient to stimulate you to want more than ever to become a loving, articulate, biblically-oriented communicator.

Scripture Index

Subject Index

Adam:
  blames Eve, 31
  restricted, 16
  seeks a companion, 17ff
Adam and Eve:
  adjustment, 21
  bi-unity relationship, 23
  broken communication with
    God, 28-29
  communication with
    God, 18-19
  discernment and decision, 18
  disobedience—separation, 26
  fall, 26
  nakedness, 21
  relationship, 21
Adaptation, 176-77
Admonishment, 107, 178, 186-89
Agnostic, 32
Alienation, 103
Alliances: with unbelievers, 172
Anger, 52, 59, 101-3, 202
Animadversion, 32ff, 171
Anxiety, 131, 135
Apology, 100
Atheist, 32

Bible. *See* Word of God
Bible study, 92
Bitterness, 211
Blessing, 102
Boasting, 183-84
Body life, 165, 188
Body language, 167

Cautious, 182
Christlikeness, 197, 210
Church discipline, 189
Church: oneness, 174-75
Cliches, 173
Cliques, 173-74
Comfort, 191-92

Communication:
  adaptive, 176-77
  audience-centered, 177
  basis of, 15
  creatively, 185
  and decisions, 22
  distorted, 26
  edification, goal of, 49
  by example, 176
  of false doctrine, 204
  with God, 16, 69ff, 75-76, 78
  with God. *See also* prayer
  hindrances to, 165ff
  in the home, 199
  honesty in, 15, 16, 90
  imperfect, 100
  learning, 54
  in marriage, 21-22
  message-center, 177
  nonverbal, 167
  with others, 78-79, 96ff,
    124-25, 148, 153, 163ff
  patterns, 128, 163, 168
  personal, 167-68
  physically, 175-76
  positive, 128
  selective in, 62ff, 173
  silence in, 48
  superficial, 173
  of truth, 59, 96, 181, 185,
    197, 206
  unwholesome, 57-58, 90
  visibly, 176
  Word of God and, 90
  and works, 168-71
Communication, God's:
  articulate, 17
  eye-to-eye, 106
  honesty in, 15
  limitation of, 96
  non-hurling, 101
  nonverbal, 167
  through others, 86-87, 107